Barbara C. Jordan
Selected Speeches

Edited by Sandra Parham

With an Introduction by
Governor Ann Richards

HOWARD UNIVERSITY PRESS
Washington, DC
1999

Howard University Press, Washington, DC 20001

Manufactured in the United States of America

This book is printed on acid-free paper.

10   9   8   7   6   5   4   3   2   1

Library of Congress Cataloging-in-Publication Data

Jordan, Barbara, 1936–
    [Speeches. Selections]
    Barbara C. Jordan—selected speeches / edited by Sandra Parham :
with a foreword by Governor Ann Richards.
        p.   cm.

    ISBN 0-88258-199-6 (acid-free paper)

    1. United States—Politics and government—1945–1989.   2. United
States—Politics and government—1989–   3. United States.
Constitution.   4. Civil rights movements—United States—
History—20th century.   5. Political ethics—United States.
I. Parham, Sandra, 1954–   . II. Title.   III. Title: Barbara C.
Jordan.   IV. Title: Selected speeches.

E838.5.J672   1999
328.73′092—dc21   99-11022
                                                                          CIP

Contents

Introduction   v

Preface   ix

Barbara Charline Jordan, 1936–1996   xi

The Barbara Jordan Archives   xv

SELECTED SPEECHES ON . . .

The Constitution   1

Nothing New Under the Sun   3

Moving on from Watergate   9

Reflections on the Constitution   15

It's More Than a Lifeless Archives   19

National Archives Address   23

Women and the Constitution: The Challenge   27

SELECTED SPEECHES ON . . .

Government and Democracy   31

The Law, the Promise, and the Power   33

In Search of Humanity   39

Civil Liberties: Inoperative? Inaudible? Unintelligible?
Expletive Deleted?   43

Can We Govern Ourselves?   49

Harvard University Commencement Address   53

Council on Foundations Keynote Address   57

SELECTED SPEECHES ON . . .
Civil Rights and Diversity   61

E Pluribus Unum: Myth or Reality? One from Many   63

How Do We Live with Each Other's
Deepest Differences?   71

Does the Idea of Civil Rights Remain a Good Idea
as We Approach the Year 2000 A.D.?   75

SELECTED SPEECHES ON . . .
Ethics   81

The Rebirth of Ethics—A Pervasive Challenge   83

Ethical Dilemmas of Leadership   89

Famous Speeches   95

Democratic National Convention Address   97

Change: From What to What?   101

Testimony Before the House Judiciary Committee
(Watergate)   105

Statement Given to *Time* Magazine on Retirement
from Congress   109

Introduction

The truth is that I had counted on Barbara Jordan's preaching my funeral . . . because she could always make anything sound better than it was. But Barbara was every bit as good as she sounded. In a world that sways on the winds of trends and polls and prognostication, she was as constant and as true as the North Star. Barbara Jordan was an American original and a national treasure. And she was my friend. I know that, at some point, I'm supposed to say that despite all the public acclaim, Barbara was really just like everyone else. But that would be wrong. No matter what else was going on, when you were with Barbara, you could never shake the feeling that you were in the presence of greatness.

I remember talking to her one time about how she prepared to teach an ethics class at the LBJ School of Public Affairs. Before Barbara's classes, ethics was not one of those courses that caused a student stampede to enroll. And the idea of actually teaching a course in ethics would have given most of us pause. But Barbara said, well, she had done her best to compile a list of everyone who had taught the course anywhere . . . and then she had written and asked each one to send her a copy of his or her syllabus. But, she said, "Of course, it was necessary for me to craft my own." And we thank God for that.

Now, if we are going to be honest, we have to say that there were some people who managed to resist Barbara's persuasive manner. When I was a county commissioner, Barbara was building her house out in the country—down at the end of a narrow, tree-shaded lane that was about a mile long. A woman who owned property along that road apparently was not thrilled to have Barbara there. So—even though the road had been open to the public forever—she had a gate put up and padlocked it. It may be hard to imagine Barbara Jordan hopping mad . . . but she was. She called me and she said, "Ann—*Ann*—this old woman put a gate across my lane. The lane is used by everyone. And I want that gate down." Well, it took no small amount of doing, but we got the lane designated for county maintenance, and we got that gate down. Years later, I asked Barbara whatever happened to that woman. Barbara suppressed a smile and got that voice of the Lord inflection in her speech. Then she said, "Uhhh . . . well, Ann, that old woman died and went to hell." And that is pretty much how it went with Barbara.

If reasoning did not work and prodding did not work and law did not work . . . divine intervention was bound to be just around the corner. People talk about what a private person Barbara was, but the American people knew everything they needed to know about her from the moment they met her. There was simply something about her that made you proud to be part of the country that produced her. Barbara gave us cause to believe in ourselves. And she forever redefined what it meant to be a Texan in the eyes of the nation. In the grimmest days of Watergate, not only was it her voice and intellect that defended the Constitution but also it was her existence. People said to themselves that if our society and our system created Barbara Jordan, then maybe there is hope. They were right.

Barbara worked hard to redeem that hope through her own public service and through her influence on the service of her students. In the chaos of political life, it is easy to forget that the horizon extends farther than the next election. Barbara never did. Her years in the Texas Senate and the Congress gave her power and fame, but those last years in Austin secured her place in history and in our hearts. The time that she spent with students—and with people like me—was important to her. And her counsel was literally invaluable to us. In politics, the tendency is to think about what someone can do for you. But there was something about Barbara that made you want to do something for her.

Stan McLelland has been Barbara's friend for a long time. And a few years ago, Stan decided Barbara needed to be able to visit him at the beach, so he went to considerable trouble and expense to have his place on South Padre Island fixed up to make it wheelchair accessible. And Barbara went down for a visit and had a great time. Then after she left, Stan and I got to worrying about how, for the next visit, we could build a boardwalk that would allow Barbara to get closer to the beach and enjoy it more. I'm not sure why she had that effect on people. Maybe it was because we knew we owed her. I like to think that Barbara knew how much she meant to us, and how grateful we are that she crafted a life that was truly her own.

When we lose someone who is dear to us, we become aware of how short the movement of life is, of how small and fragile we are in this ocean of time. Our loss today is personal and it is profound. Our friend, our sister, our daughter is gone. But Barbara Jordan is still with us—and she is strong. There is nothing small or fragile about her legacy. It will thrive, and she will live on through us—the people who admired her and learned from her and loved her.

We know that, in the words of that old gospel song, she lifted us to higher ground. And we thank God for the glory of her life . . . and the pleasure and the honor of her company.

Ann Richards
(From her remarks at the funeral
service of Barbara Jordan)

Preface

This book is a selection of speeches by the late Barbara Jordan. They span the period from 1967 through 1995. The book represents only a small portion of the speeches and interviews she gave throughout an illustrious career.

The aim of this book is to present some of the major ideas Jordan expounded and defended during her lifetime. The subjects of these speeches represent Jordan's philosophy on diversity, the Constitution, ethics, and government, as well as those speeches for which Jordan is best known: the Senate Judiciary Hearing Speech, commonly referred to as the Watergate Speech; and the 1976 and 1992 Democratic National Convention speeches, among others. Convinced that Jordan will be the subject of much study by historians, scholars, and students in years to come, we believe that the present book will serve as an invaluable source of material for their studies.

Jordan was an extraordinary speaker and writer. The printed speeches do not convey adequately her remarkable qualities as a speaker and the effect they had on the audience. The explanatory notes accompanying the speeches are intended to indicate where and when they were given, with no interpretive or editorial comment.

Barbara Jordan exemplified integrity. She left lessons of determination, tenacity, and ethical responsibility for all who follow in her path. She will be missed.

Barbara Charline Jordan 1936–1996

Barbara Charline Jordan, dynamic orator, legislator, and educator, has left an indelible mark on our times. Her journey—from the segregated Fifth Ward Houston of her childhood to her becoming a legendary public figure on the international stage—was filled with a series of "firsts."

Barbara Jordan was born on February 21, 1936. Graduating with honors from Houston's Phillis Wheatley High School, she went on to Texas Southern University (TSU), where she majored in government and history. While in college, Jordan refined her oratorical skills by becoming a member of the renowned TSU Debate Team. After graduating magna cum laude from TSU in 1956, she attended the Boston University Law School.

Following her graduation from law school in 1959, Barbara Jordan served as administrative assistant to the county judge of Harris County, the first Black woman ever to hold that position. She was later elected to the Texas State Senate in 1966, the first Black elected to the Senate since 1883.

On January 3, 1973, Jordan was sworn in as a member of the 93d Congress. Jordan was thirty-six years old. She was the first representative from the newly created Eighteenth Congressional District of Texas, becoming the first Black Texan in the U.S. Congress.

Jordan's legend grew quickly. She had the reputation of being a skilled and forceful politician. She took the advice of her good friend, former President Lyndon Johnson, and asked for service on the House Judiciary Committee. Because of her overwhelming competence and the intervention of friends, she received the cherished assignment that soon thrust her into the national limelight. During the 1974 House Judiciary Committee hearing on Watergate,

Jordan had the ear of the world as she delivered her impassioned speech on impeachment and the Constitution.

Two years later Jordan claimed another significant first. She delivered the keynote address at the 1976 Democratic Party Convention, the first Black woman to do so in the 144-year history of the organization. This historic speech launched her into the ranks of the political elite.

During her three terms in the House, Jordan served on both the Judiciary and Government Operations Committees and the Steering and Policy Committee of the Democratic Caucus. She was also instrumental in passing key amendments to the Voting Rights Act and in establishing mandatory Civil Rights Act enforcement procedures for the Law Enforcement Assistance Administration and the Office of Revenue Sharing.

Barbara Jordan made the decision to end her political career in December 1977. She chose her next career path in academics and accepted a post at the Lyndon Baines Johnson School of Public Affairs at the University of Texas. She stated that she wanted to help train the future leaders of the nation and to bring government back to the people. She believed that people in government should be held to the highest ethical standard. With this philosophy, she became ethics adviser to former Texas Governor Ann Richards.

Jordan's accomplishments and accolades span her lifetime. In 1966, she was named Outstanding Freshman Senator of the Texas Senate. In 1972, she was honored by the Texas Senate by being named Governor for a Day. In 1974, she was given the Sojourner Truth Award from the Black Women's Development Foundation. In 1975, she was elected Woman of the Year by the Women's National Democratic Club. In 1976, she was named as one of the ten Women of the Year by *Time* magazine. In 1977, Phillis Wheatley High School designated her as its Outstanding Graduate, and she was named to *Good Housekeeping* magazine's ten most admired women, an honor she repeated the following year. *World Almanac* listed her as one of the twenty-five most influential women in America in each year from 1974 through 1984. *Redbook* named her first in performance among congressional women in 1978. In 1984, she was elected to the Texas Women's Hall of Fame, received the Eleanor Roosevelt Humanities Award, was given the Distinguished Alumnus Award by the American Association of State Colleges and Universities, and was inducted into the Orators Hall of Fame. She was the recipient of the Tom C. Clark Equal Justice Under the Law Award in 1991 and was inducted into the African American Hall of Fame in 1993.

Jordan continued to contribute to the American political sphere after being appointed to chair the U.S. Commission on Immigration Reform in 1993. She received more than thirty honorary doctorates from such prestigious institutions as Harvard, Princeton, Howard, and her alma mater, Texas Southern

University. In the summer of 1994, she was awarded the Presidential Medal of Freedom, the highest civilian award in the land.

Barbara Jordan achieved a kind of immortality not because of her numerous awards and honors, but because of her legacy of public service. She will live on in the hearts and minds of the young people she touched in her final profession.

Barbara Charline Jordan died January 17, 1996, at the age of fifty-nine. She was buried at the State Cemetery in Austin, Texas, near the grave of Stephen Austin, the "father of Texas." Her final first in the series of firsts achieved in her lifetime—she is believed to be the first Black to be buried in the Texas State Cemetery.

She will be missed.

Sandra Parham

The Barbara Jordan Archives

The establishment of the Barbara Jordan Archives at Texas Southern University was an extraordinary gift from one of the most outstanding alumnae of the University. When then-Representative Jordan opted to retire from Congress in 1978, the University finalized negotiations to become the repository for the records of her career. On August 16, 1978, Representative Jordan officially deposited her papers with the Texas Southern University Library.

The collection of Jordan's papers, manuscripts, and personal memorabilia originally spanned the period from 1967 through 1978. However, Jordan discovered that though she had retired from Congress, she had not retired from public life. She continued to receive many outstanding tributes and awards and still actively contributed to the political sphere by writing, speaking, and serving as adviser to Texas Governor Ann Richards. The collection of "citizen" Jordan's material continued to expand as she donated all of it to the archives until her death on January 17, 1996.

The archives now include memorabilia from Jordan's early years at Phyllis Wheatley High School, her time at Texas Southern University, and her career as an attorney in Houston. The congressional collection includes her remarks on the floor of the House, records from the Judiciary Committee hearings, bills she introduced, legislative and other correspondence, all office files, and numerous speeches. The final phase of the collection incorporates the many speeches she delivered after leaving public office, the countless awards and trophies bestowed during her lifetime, the videotapes of interviews and speeches, an extensive library, and a tremendous file of photographs documenting a lifetime of achievements.

The University takes great pride in its responsibility as custodian of this living legacy. Our pledge is to make available this wealth of documents bequeathed by one of the nation's most admired citizens of the twentieth century, Barbara Charline Jordan.

Barbara Jordan being sworn in by Judge Andrew Jefferson as Governor for a Day. Photo by Earlie Hudnall. Reprinted by permission of Texas Southern University Archives.

Swearing in as a member of the 93d Congress. January 3, 1973. Photo by Dev O'Neill. Reprinted by permission of Texas Southern University Archives.

Signing of the Voting Rights Act. September 4, 1974. Reprinted by permission of Texas Southern University Archives.

December 12, 1972. Photo by Frank Wolfe. Reprinted by permission of Texas Southern University Archives.

Photo by Dev O'Neill. Reprinted by permission of Texas Southern University Archives.

October 5, 1974. Photo by Dev O'Neill. Reprinted by permission of Texas Southern University Archives.

Reprinted by permission of Texas Southern University Archives.

Democratic National Committee Mini Convention. Kansas City. July 1975. Photo by Dev O'Neill. Reprinted by permission of Texas Southern University Archives.

University of Notre Dame. 1975. Reprinted by permission of Texas Southern University Archives.

Viewing the Magna Carta. 1976. Photo by Dev O'Neill. Reprinted by permission of Texas Southern University Archives.

House Judiciary Committee. 1978. Photo by Dev O'Neill. Reprinted by permission of Texas Southern University Archives.

Barbara Jordan and Austin Symphony conductor, Sung Kwan. 1992. Reprinted by permission of Texas Southern University Archives.

The Constitution

Barbara Jordan's loyalty to, belief in, and defense of the United States Constitution is nationally heralded. The many speeches in which she referred to the Constitution are testimony to her now famous quote, "My faith in the Constitution is whole, it is complete, it is total. . . ." The following speeches, "Nothing New Under the Sun," "Moving on from Watergate," "Reflections on the Constitution" and "It's More Than a Lifeless Archives," all exemplify Jordan as a scholar and a student of the Constitution.

The final two speeches in this section, remarks given at the National Archives and at the Women and the Constitution: A Bicentennial Perspective Symposium, examine Jordan's strong views on the void of women in the Constitution.

My faith in the Constitution is whole; it is complete; it is total.
I am not going to sit here and be an idle spectator to the
diminution, the subversion, the destruction of the Constitution.

Testimony before the House Judiciary Committee
JULY 25, 1974

Nothing New Under the Sun

Throughout the history of our country, it has not been un-usual for Americans—politicians and nonpoliticians alike—to herald the nobility of our country's purpose and ideals. Witness the debate over whether the Congress should provide aid for the assistance of Vietnamese refugees. The responsibility of this country to solve a problem it helped to create was not sharply focused. Rather, the words etched on the Statue of Liberty were invoked: tired, poor, huddled masses longing to breathe free. At its very first session, the Continental Congress in 1774 approved the so-called Declaration of Rights in the form of ten resolutions stating the *fundamental* rights which the colonies held were theirs—rights derived from "the immutable laws of nature, the principles of the English constitution, and the several charters or compacts" (an example of nobility in pronouncement which was ignored). The Second Continental Congress assembled in 1775 and was not bereft of eloquent tongues. It resolved "that a general be appointed to command all the continental forces, raised or to be raised, for the defense of American liberty." "Rights" and "liberties" became the staple ingredients of those early debates and documents, which were the forerunners of the Declaration of Independence and the Constitution of the United States. The participants in those congresses were primarily concerned with immediate relief from tyranny. They could not express a world view nor total humanitarian view, for their experience was confined to the well-being of a sovereignty of thirteen tiny colonies. The passionate distaste for tyranny and ardent desire for independence [are] a credible legacy forwarded to us by the first Americans.

It is for us to seize the lessons of history and give substance and reality to purposes, goals, and ideals so nobly expressed. The transition from sound, fury, and dreams to fact has not been an easy one. We have been in transition for almost 200 years, and the path remains fraught with travail.

As we approach the celebration of our nation's bicentennial, we are really celebrating the confluence of two events: the statement of liberty embodied in the Declaration of Independence and the Constitution's creation of democratic institutions devised to guard our liberties. Having always had both the Declaration of Independence and the Constitution to study, we sometimes forget that the two documents are not the same. The Declaration expresses only the principles and sentiments of liberty, freedom, and justice. It is silent on what form of government should be instituted to guarantee those sentiments. Historians have noted that the uniqueness of the American Revolution stems partially from the fact that the American colonies did not, when declaring war with the Crown, have a specific form of national government in mind. In fact, among many leaders of the era, it was assumed that once independence was secured, the colonies would act as thirteen sovereign states. This view nearly prevailed. The Confederacy was the embodiment of the prevailing view that a central government strong enough to compel action was not what the revolution was all about. The devisement of a central government was not pre-planned.

Americans made their quest for liberty in 1776, but it was not until 1787 that they created a democratic republic. After having muddled through a wholly ineffective confederacy, the delegates in Philadelphia struggled with the dilemma of whether to tinker with the old instrument or begin anew.

The decision to start anew was spawned as much by frustration with what was—the Articles of Confederation—as by the wish to create institutions which would secure individual liberties. The delegates cast off upon uncharted waters; there was greater unanimity about the governmental harbor they sought to create than about the navigational chart.

From our vantage point nearly 200 years later, we tend to focus on the document that *emerged* from their deliberations and to assume that the best form of government is democratic. We further assume that the delegates immediately set their sights on the creation of a democracy. Not so. For the constitutional delegates, the task was to translate the eloquently expressed principles of the Declaration of Independence to a practicable *modus operandi*. What Pericles said of the Athenians also characterized the venture of the delegates: "We do not imitate—for we are a model to others."

Many of the eventual signatories of the Constitution were more fearful of the potential disadvantages of a democratic form of government than they were enthusiastic about the potential advantages. Rampant democracy could result in anarchy. For other delegates, concern for the ensurance of individual liberties eclipsed their apprehension about the possibility of the exercise of those liberties to extreme. Many thought that a democratic form of government was at best exceedingly risky and in constant need of scrutiny. Democracy had a chance of working only through the creation of countervailing institutions designed to mitigate potential dangers.

That which has proven to be the oldest federal constitution in existence contained the ingenious governmental structure that has functioned for nearly two centuries: three institutions with enumerated powers, autonomous yet complementary, each jealous of its constitutional prerogatives and sensitive to the possible malfeasance or nonfeasance of its co-partners.

The Constitution, then, created the institutions of government, designed to be forever at odds with one another in order that the democratic republic could withstand the competing forces of society, such as revolution versus order, individual liberty versus tyranny, human rights versus property rights. These conflicts have been with us since the beginning of this nation. They continue to divide us today. As we seek to develop solutions to these issues, we are continuing to consecrate the seeds of our democratic republic.

Understandably, our attention is typically focused on contemporary issues. Many of the conflicts which have so long divided us are not without current counterparts. The busing of school children is just such an issue. It arouses passions; it is both local and national in scope. Some characterize the issue as local control of our educational system versus national control. Many colonists fought passionately against the ratification of the Constitution because they were fearful that local autonomy would be jeopardized. Others characterize the busing issue as one relating to enforcement of the equal protection clause of the Fourteenth Amendment of the Constitution. Regardless of the side you may take, the busing issue is a struggle to continue to extend the ideals of American democracy to those formerly in bondage. Where cruelty and injustice exist, there will always, I hope, be those who will articulate the ideals of American democracy in an endeavor to press for their individual and collective liberties.

The Constitution has further protected democracy from itself by the creation of a judiciary not directly responsible to popular will. Without the constant prodding of the judiciary, we might not have begun the task of grappling with the problems that were caused by and resulted from unequal educational opportunity. If we are to honor the principles of liberty in the Declaration of Independence and the principles of equality in the Constitution, it is mandatory—it is morally mandatory—that the judiciary continue to disassemble the barrier to racial equality.

The colonists knew that tyrants and despots were perpetuated in office through an inherent right of hereditary succession. This practice was anathema to a democracy and violative of individual freedoms. The laws which sanctioned this practice were repealed. The right of the individual to pursue unencumbered the destiny of his choice provided the basic rationale for many anti-poverty and social welfare programs in 1957.

Religious freedom so permanently established by the Constitution is yet another example of the type of issues which continue to face us today. Two hundred years ago, the issue was the right of an individual to hold and express views of his conscience. Does the current abortion controversy not have similar philosophical underpinnings?

The issues from the social revolution of the 1770s to the issues of the civil rights revolution of the 1960s can be directly traceable. Both are attempts to fulfill the American ideals of a democratic republic.

Our nation is destined to constantly grapple with the basic paradoxes faced by the Founding Fathers. Each one of us is continually involved. We cannot escape the fact that neither the Declaration of Independence nor the Constitution solves the inherent problems of democracy. And we must pay it constant attention.

We cannot disenthrall ourselves from history nor should we ignore it. As President Truman said, "The only thing new in the world is the history you don't know." It does not contribute to the quality of the debate for us to recite the long train of abuses suffered by some of the citizens of this country. Nor is it helpful to highlight the incongruity of the actions and rhetoric of America. Our job is to make the match.

The truths were then and are now more self-evident than the means of implementing them. So it was in 1787 and so it is today. The issues before us in 1975, just as issues in the past and in the future, require the thoughtful consideration of all Americans who refuse to take lightly their responsibilities as citizens.

The economic issues confronting us today evidence the seeming inconsistency of a $1.5 trillion economy concurrent with a 9 percent rate of unemployment and a declining rate of real production.

The prospect of another oil embargo forces us to recognize our vulnerability to the policies of other nations. The finiteness of our *own* natural resources should force us to focus on the development and effects of our own policies.

We are discomfited by poverty and hunger silhouetted against wealth and abundance. We are bewildered by illiteracy juxtaposed with a knowledge explosion. We are at once sick and well, rich and poor.

I think it neither a subtle nor accidental distinction that the Declaration of Independence states, "*We* hold these truths to be self-evident," rather than "These truths are held to be self-evident," and that the Constitution states, "*We* the people of the United States," rather than "The people of the United States." The word "*We*" contemplates the emplacement of people to make actionable our basic documents and the precepts they espouse. We the people—the elected and the electorate—are both heirs and trustees, beneficiaries and benefactors. It has always been that way.

With dedicated vigilance, firm resolve, and divine guidance, in the third century of the life of this country, we may raise a standard heralding the triumph of liberty over tyranny, order over revolution, and meaning over emptiness.

The quality of your life will determine whether that standard bespeaks the truth or whether it does also lie.

Texas Law Review *Annual Banquet*
Driskill Hotel, Austin, Texas
MARCH 8, 1975

Moving on from Watergate

On Tuesday, August 20, 1974, the House of Representatives accepted from its Committee on the Judiciary a privileged report on impeachment. That report recommended "that the House exercise its constitutional power to impeach Richard M. Nixon, President of the United States, and that articles of impeachment be exhibited to the Senate. . . ."

But for his own precipitous resignation, the recommendations of the committee would have been adopted by the House. But for a simple letter tendered to the Secretary of State, he would have been found guilty in the Senate.

After reviewing 650 statements of information and 7,200 pages of supporting evidentiary materials, the Judiciary Committee came to some conclusions. Richard Nixon, *a lawyer*, had committed impeachable acts, high crimes, and misdemeanors. Richard Nixon, who graduated from Duke Law School with honors, had failed his own oath: ". . . to the best of my ability to preserve, protect, and defend the Constitution of the United States." Richard Nixon, admitted to the bar in 1937, violated his constitutional duty to take care that the laws be faithfully executed. Richard Nixon, the committee agreed, had committed crimes against our Constitution.

Twenty-two other lawyers have been found guilty of statutory crimes, both civil and criminal, in furtherance of Mr. Nixon's designs: John Mitchell, Attorney General, guilty. Richard Kleindienst, Attorney General, guilty. John Dean, Legal Counsel to the President, guilty. Herb Kalmbach, personal lawyer to the President, guilty. John Ehrlichman, Legal Counsel and Domestic Affairs Adviser, guilty. Guilty also are Charles Colson, Egil Krogh, Gordon Liddy, Robert Mardian, Kenneth Parkinson, Harry Sears, Donald Segretti, David Young—all lawyers.

The Watergate drama did not leave lawyers totally guilty of complicity. We have our heroes: Elliot Richardson, Archibald Cox, Leon Jaworski, John Sirica, Peter Rodino, John Doar, and Albert Jenner. Even among Republican defenders of the President there stood honorable men who would not defend his actions in the face of clear and convincing evidence of constitutional crimes. But in its aftermath, we should not create yet another cover-up. That a panel of lawyers made the impeachment clause work during this century, or that a shaky band of stalwarts would not buckle under pressure from the most powerful man in the world, should not deter us from driving from our midst those who misbehaved, who betrayed their oath to uphold the rule of law. Lawyers have a special responsibility to act within the law. Those who operate outside its boundaries should properly remain outside the practice of the legal profession.

The impeachment clause of the Constitution has been shown to reach a President grown tyrannical and swollen with power. I foresee no means by which it can be improved. But for other offenses, committed by other men, constant vigilance and intense public scrutiny of the public's business are our best safeguards. Beyond vigilance and scrutiny, other actions can and should be taken to correct the abuses of Watergate. But care should be taken that we learn our lesson well—that we not misunderstand Watergate.

I am somewhat reluctant to use parts of the Watergate drama as a model of evil. As a model, for instance, the break-in at the Democratic National Committee headquarters on the night of June 17, 1972, fails every elementary test. Even the unflappable Tony Ulasewicz recognized it as comic opera. "I will tell you, any old retired man in the New York City Police Department who would become involved in a thing like that . . . he would not have walked in with an army, that is for sure. He probably would have walked in like any decent, common-looking citizen; laid something in the right place; and walked right out and that would have been the end of it for a long time."

I would add that Mr. Ulasewicz would probably not have walked in with identification papers, serial numbered $100 bills, nor an address book.

Although it may delight our fancies that such straight Republicans would employ court jesters, the Judiciary Committee chronicled enough abuses to fill the legislative hoppers with proposed solutions for many Congresses. For some abuses, I hope we have already minimized their future occurrences. For others, we must continue to seek correcting legislation.

In the articles of impeachment, the committee found the President had maintained the cover-up by "approving and acquiescing in the surreptitious payment of substantial sums of money for the purpose of obtaining the silence or influencing the testimony of witnesses" (Article I, Section 5). And further, the committee found Richard Nixon had "authorized and permitted to be maintained a secret investigative unit within the office of the President, financed in part with money derived from campaign contributions, which engaged in covert and unlawful activities, and attempted to prejudice the constitutional right of an accused to a fair trial."

To some extent, the Watergate problem was a problem of too much cash: Cash from corporations, cash funneled through dummy committees. Cash in envelopes, cash in satchels and briefcases. Cash left in mail boxes, cash left in telephone booths. Cash kept in White House safes, cash distributed indiscriminately. For a seemingly interminable list of surreptitious projects, a seemingly endless supply of cash.

Principally as the result of this experience, Congress passed last October the Campaign Finance Reform Act. It simply bars cash contributions of over $100. It limits to $1,000 the amount an individual may give to a candidate in each primary, runoff, and general election. It requires candidates to establish one central campaign committee through which all contributions and expenditures on behalf of a candidate must be reported. It requires designation of specific bank depositories of campaign funds. It requires full reports of contributions and expenditures to be filed. And the law is to be enforced by a newly created eight-member, independent, full-time, bipartisan Federal Elections Commission. Cash will no longer be a problem.

Other abuses detailed by the impeachment investigation are only now receiving attention in the Congress. Once again, the articles of impeachment: Richard Nixon sought to obstruct justice by "endeavoring to misuse the Central Intelligence Agency" (Article I, Section 6). And further, "He has, acting personally and through his subordinates and agents, endeavored to obtain from the Internal Revenue Service, in violation of the constitutional rights of citizens, confidential information . . ." (Article II, Section 1). He misused the FBI and Secret Service for purposes unrelated to national security (Article II, Section 2).

In part, as the result of Nixon's misuse of the CIA and FBI and, in part, as the result of disclosures in recent months, both the House and Senate have created special committees charged with investigating our so-called national security intelligence agencies. In addition, there is pending in the House Judiciary Committee a bill which would place strict limits on the volume and type of information which law enforcement agencies may tender to other government agencies.

Immediately preceding the House Judiciary Committee's impeachment investigation, the House Government Operations Committee documented that at least $17 million of public funds were spent on Mr. Nixon's seaside villas. In response, the House passed last year a bill providing for greater accountability by the Secret Service on funds it spends to protect the President, his family, and other high officials. Unfortunately, the bill was not considered in the Senate and thus died at the end of the last Congress. It will be considered again by the House in a few weeks.

Pending also in Congress are bills, among them one of my own, which would provide a mechanism whereby federal district courts, at the request of grand juries, may appoint special prosecutors. The cover-up was successful for a period of time because of the failure of the discovery and investigatory processes of the criminal justice system. For the future we need a mechanism whereby the investigators are not beholden to the investigated. When the conduct of executive branch officials is in question, grand juries should be able to retain special prosecutors [that are] not a part of the executive branch.

Pervading the entire Watergate episode were allegations the President's power had swollen beyond reasonable proportions. The President tried to withhold from the Congress information not related to national defense on the basis of executive privilege. Now the Senate rules provide that each presidential appointee, in order to secure confirmation, must answer affirmatively that all information requested by the Congress from the appointee's office will be provided unless specifically withheld by the President to protect against foreign enemies.

The President, in 1973, tried to institute a series of impoundments which effectively killed numerous programs thought worthy of continued existence by the Congress. In response, the Congress passed the Budget and Impoundment Control Act. It not only establishes a totally congressional budget office but also provides procedures whereby the Congress may formally disapprove of presidential impoundments. And having done so, the President is obliged to spend the funds.

The unilateral commitment of United States military forces in Southeast Asia prompted the Congress to enact, over the President's veto, the War Powers Act. Now the President may not commit troops to overseas combat for more than sixty days without the express approval of the Congress.

And finally, the House Judiciary Committee has begun hearings on a lengthy bill which would repeal many of the so-called emergency powers granted to the President but never exercised. Utilizing the principle that delegated power which is not employed is unjust power, the Congress will be seeking to prevent future Presidents from justifying a wild scheme based upon an obscure nineteenth-century statute.

None of these congressional actions can overcome the most basic Watergate problem. Neither the House Judiciary Committee's investigation, [nor] a vote in both the House and Senate, nor the forced removal of a President would have protected us against moral ineptitude. Decency, integrity, honor, honesty—these cannot be legislated. The Congress is ill equipped to amend the Ten Commandments. And should it try, it would probably create some loopholes which are not there now. A government of a thousand laws cannot overcome one man's will to chastise his neighbor.

And yet, the torment of Watergate is a sign to us all.

We have both the capacity and the will to act within our democratic institutions to right our wrongs.

We have the requisite mechanisms to protect our liberties from violation. As James Madison said:

> It is proper to take alarm at the first experiment on our liberties. We hold this prudent jealousy to be the first duty of citizens, and one of the noblest characteristics of the late Revolution. The freemen of America did not wait till usurped power had strengthened itself by exercise, and entangled the question in precedents. They saw all the consequences in the principle, and they avoided the consequences by denying the principle.

We know, moreover, our Constitution has withstood the threats of the past and holds every promise of doing so in the future. We know this because we have examined its roots and found them to be firm.

Article for The Houston Lawyer
JULY 14, 1987

Reflections on
the Constitution

The nation's only Black Supreme Court Justice, Thurgood Marshall, gave a speech recently which sparked much discussion and debate. In speaking of the 200th anniversary celebration of the United States Constitution, Mr. Justice Marshall said,

> The focus of this celebration invites the complacent belief that the vision of those who debated and compromised in Philadelphia yielded the "more perfect union" it is said we now enjoy. I cannot accept this invitation, for I do not believe that the meaning of the Constitution was forever "fixed" at the Philadelphia Convention. Nor do I find the wisdom, foresight, and sense of justice exhibited by the Framers particularly profound. To the contrary, the government they devised was defective from the start, requiring several amendments, a civil war, and momentous social transformation to attain the system of constitutional government and its respect for the individual freedoms and human rights [that] we hold as fundamental today. When contemporary Americans cite "the Constitution," they invoke a concept that is vastly different from what the Framers barely began to construct two centuries ago.

I considered thoughtfully what the Justice had said and recalled my own words spoken during the impeachment proceedings of Richard Nixon. I had said, "We the People" is an eloquent beginning to the Constitution. But for a long time I had thought the Framers left me out by mistake. However, through the process of amendment and court action, I have finally been included in "We the People." I then added, "My faith in the Constitution is whole. It is complete. It is total." That was my faith in 1974 and it remains my faith in 1987.

I celebrate the bicentennial of the Constitution and do not believe that to be a celebrant you must believe that the meaning of the Constitution was forever fixed at the Philadelphia Convention. I couldn't believe that. I know it was no mistake to leave women and Blacks out of the Constitution. It was a deliberate omission.

The original language of Article I, Section 2, Paragraph 3, of the Constitution states, "Representatives and direct taxes shall be apportioned among the several states which may be included within this union, according to their respective numbers, which shall be determined by adding to the whole number of free persons, including those bound to service for a term of years and excluding Indians not taxed, three-fifths of all other persons." "Three-fifths of all other persons." That phrase includes my ancestors. If the original meaning had been fixed forever, I would today count as three-fifths of a person. Section 2 of the Fourteenth Amendment to the Constitution changed that. It states, "Representatives shall be apportioned among the several states according to their respective numbers, counting the whole number of persons in each state, excluding Indians not taxed." This amendment was proposed by Congress on June 13, 1866. It was ratified by July 28, 1868. The document signed by the Framers on September 17, 1787, was not immutable. It provided a framework—a structure for governing. As many of the drafters campaigned for ratification, they promised that several amendments would be added which would make the Constitution more acceptable. James Madison is generally regarded as the father of the Constitution. One of his first acts as a member of Congress was to propose amending the Constitution to add a Bill of Rights. James Madison was fulfilling a campaign promise.

Did the fact of adding the first ten amendments to the Constitution so soon after ratification mean that the instrument as ratified was defective? There was no unanimous answer to that question. Strong advocates of the natural rights of man felt that a Bill of Rights was unnecessary because it constituted only a restatement of rights already held by man by virtue of being human. Ardent antifederalists, ever distrustful of government, felt that a Bill of Rights was necessary to protect the citizenry from encroachment and intrusion by big government. It is my belief that those first ten amendments to the Constitution provide a cogent and concise statement of this country's public philosophy. They are a convenient and substantive response to what this country is about.

Those first ten amendments applied to the federal government and its constitutional restraints. The question of whether those amendments were applicable to the states was answered by the decision that the Fourteenth Amendment incorporated the first ten amendments and made them applicable to the states. With that, the whole of government was constitutionally enjoined from interfering with those basic freedoms of speech, press, religion, conscience, thought, and assembly.

In the early sixties, I sought election in Houston. There were twelve representatives from Houston-Harris County to be elected to the Texas House of Representatives. I wanted to be one of them. There were no single-member districts. To get elected, it was necessary to run countywide and receive a majority vote. I lost such an election in 1962 and 1964. Subsequent to those races, a constitutional question was raised in federal court about the fairness of such at-large elections. Ultimately a Supreme Court decision styled *Baker v. Carr* held such elections unconstitutional and ordered redistricting by the state legislature. In 1966 I ran for election to the state senate from one of the newly created districts and won. It was the Constitution of the United States embodying the principle of equal representation which made it possible for me to attain office.

To this point, I have mentioned amendments and court decisions which stretched the Constitution to include me. An understandable next question is whether the product of the Philadelphia Convention contained anything which could stand the test of time unaltered and unamended. The answer is an unequivocal yes.

1. We have a republican form of government in which the people are sovereign.
2. Our government is organized into three co-equal branches which check and balance each other.
3. The doctrine of separation of powers underlies the government to better secure the liberties of the people.
4. No king or monarch can come to power in America.
5. This is a government of laws wherein the rule of law prevails.
6. The Constitution and all laws made in pursuance of it are declared to be the supreme law of the land.
7. We are a union of states.

All that and much more constitute the "Miracle at Philadelphia." I am an unabashed and proud celebrant of the Constitution of the United States.

It's More Than
a Lifeless Archives

It was on this date 200 years ago that the convention which had assembled to draft the Constitution of the United States of America concluded its deliberations. That convention had begun its work in late May. The summer had been hot and the debate at times rancorous. And now the motion was made for adding the last formula, "Done in convention by the unanimous consent," etc., which was agreed to and added accordingly. The deed had been done. The compromises had been made. And now it was up to the people in the various states to approve of this Constitution in ratifying conventions held for that purpose. The people did so ratify and the government of the United States of America was reborn.

The drafters of the Constitution knew what kind of government they had created. That is, they knew that this government was a grand experiment such as had not been tried by others. The Framers explicitly rejected a monarchy and included in the text of Article I the provision that "no title of nobility shall be granted by the United States." It had only been eleven years since the Declaration of Independence cited the long train of abuses [that] the colonists had suffered under the reign of King George III. The United States was placing its trust in the people to govern. This fact finds reinforcement in Section 4 of Article 4 of the Constitution, which states, "The United States shall guarantee to every state in this Union a republican form of Government." Because the people govern, the citizen has an obligation and duty (responsibility?) to become informed about the activities of the government and let his elected representative know how he feels about what he or she is doing. The officials who have authority to make decisions in the government have it *only* because the people consent for them to have that authority. The people have the right to

20   *Barbara Jordan: Selected Speeches*

withdraw their consent and choose other decision makers if they desire. That is the meaning, the essence, of a republican form of government. As new Americans, it is my hope that you will be ever attentive of your responsibility for governing.

The Framers of the Constitution were passionate about freedom. (I do not here deal with the issue of slavery.) They were well aware of the capacity of government to oppress and burden. In fact, their experiences had made them distrustful of government and caused them to put in place checks on governmental power. The three branches of the government—legislative, executive, and judicial—are coequal, and check and balance each other. In this way, one branch may not become so powerful that it endangers the liberties of the people. We are protected from the excesses of any one branch of government. This remarkable document, the Constitution, contains that inherent protection of the liberties of the people.

So how could slavery *not* be addressed in the face of this concern for freedom? If slavery had been declared illegal in the Constitution, the southern states would have withdrawn, and no union, perfect or imperfect, would have been possible. That issue was postponed to be dealt with at another time and place. The wrenching pain of a civil war was necessary to resolve the issue, but the union survived and prevailed. The union was a part of the Constitutional Convention's miracle.

As the campaign for ratification of the Constitution got under way, opposition to the document surfaced because it did not contain a Bill of Rights. James Madison, who is regarded by many as the father of the Constitution, promised that as a member of Congress he would propose and shepherd through to passage a Bill of Rights. He did. And by 1791 the Bill of Rights had been added to the Constitution, guaranteeing American citizens freedom of religion, speech, press, conscience, assembly, and association, among others. The people may have had these freedoms as a matter of natural rights and state constitutional protections, but suspicions about the long reach of government moved the Congress to approve the Bill of Rights as the first ten amendments to the Constitution.

The work which was concluded on this day 200 years ago was of unmatched importance in the history of mankind. Fifty-five men gathered to give birth to a national government which would become the crown jewel of freedom around the world. Thirty-eight remained to sign the document. Was it perfect? No one said that it was. Benjamin Franklin made a final speech to the convention. In it he said,

> I doubt, too, whether any other convention we can obtain may be able to make a better constitution; for when you assemble a number of men to have the advantage of their joint wisdom, you inevitably assemble with those men all their prejudices, their passions, their errors of opinion, their local

interests, and their selfish views. From such an assembly can a perfect production be expected? It therefore astonished me, sir, to find this system approaching so near to perfection as it does. . . . Thus I consent, sir, to this Constitution because I expect no better, and because I am not sure that it is not the best.

Two hundred years later, I am not sure that it is not the best. The Constitution is alive and well in America. It is not a lifeless piece of paper resting in a dusty archives. It is a living document, and what brings it to life is you, the citizens of this country who will live out its meaning. You give it life— much, much more than a lifeless archives.

National Archives Address

Thank you for inviting me to say something on the occasion of this significant anniversary of one of history's most delayed and essential events. As a nation not yet born, one word in contrast to all others evoked deep emotion and an unfocused apprehension. Equality. That word, with its elusive meaning, dogged relentlessly the ideas of the late eighteenth century. Men of light and learning sought to create a new nation "dedicated to the proposition that all men are created equal." They crafted with beautiful prose documents that incorporated their ideas: the Declaration of Independence; the Constitution of the United States; its addendum, the Bill of Rights. Great documents. Great words . . . with a concomitantly great void. Those words applied almost exclusively to white males of Anglo-Saxon descent who owned property on the East Coast. A change was both necessary and obvious.

The first order of business was to get the Constitution ratified. Alexander Hamilton, James Madison, and John Jay wrote a series of essays explaining and defending the Constitution. These became, as you know, *The Federalist Papers*. Was any attempt made to explain those glaring omissions? No. That most meaningful exposition of our origins gives not one hint that women lived and should have a role in deciding how they lived. The one woman we all read about in American history was Abigail Adams. In her letter to her husband, John, on March 31, 1776, she wrote,

> In the new code of laws which I suppose it will be necessary for you to make, I desire you would remember the ladies and be more generous and favorable to them than your ancestors. Do not put such unlimited power into the hands of the husbands. Remember, all men would be tyrants if they could. If particular care and attention is not paid to the ladies we are

23

determined to form a rebellion, and will not hold ourselves bound by any laws in which we have not voice or representation.

Those were words both feisty and revolutionary. Did her words have consequences? Immediately? No. Ultimately? Yes. It is a long way from 1776 to 1920. But metamorphoses occurred and change happened. Women were not comatose during all of those years, and the idea of equality continued to resonate. Just as this nation could not survive half slave and half free, this democracy could not survive with the franchise only extended to one-half its citizenry.

Susan B. Anthony, Elizabeth Cady Stanton, and Lucretia Mott were alive and well and pushing this nation to extend the right to vote to women. That we are here for this event is eloquent testimony of their success. A marble statue of them lies in the basement of the Capitol. There have been efforts to move the statue upstairs to the Rotunda. They have failed. The statue of the suffragists was presented to Congress seventy-four years ago. May it be deemed worthy to join the gentlemen shown in Statuary Hall before another three-quarters of a century has passed.

The voices on behalf of this essential and basic right were not monochromatic. A tall, gaunt, Black woman made one of the most eloquent speeches presented to the Women's Rights Convention in Akron, Ohio, on May 29, 1851. Her name was Sojourner Truth. She said,

Well, childern, where there is so much racket there must be something out o'kilter. I think that 'twixt the negroes of the South and the women at the North, all talkin' 'bout rights, the white men will be in a fix pretty soon. But what's all this here talkin' 'bout?

That man over there say that women needs to be helped into carriages, and lifted over ditches, and to have the best place everywhere. Nobody ever helps me into carriages, or over mud-puddles, or gives me any best place! And ain't I a woman?

Look at me! Look at my arm! I have ploughed and planted, and gathered into barns, and no man could head me! And ain't I a woman?

I could work as much and eat as much as a man—when I could get it—and bear the lash as well! And ain't I a woman?

I have borne thirteen childern, and seen them most all sold off to slavery, and when I cried out with my mother's grief, none but Jesus heard me! And ain't I a woman?

Then they talks 'bout this thing in the head; what do they call it? ("Intellect" whispered someone near.) That's it, honey. What's that got to do with women's rights or negro rights? If my cup won't hold but a pint, and yours holds a quart, wouldn't you be mean not to let me have my little half-measure full?

Then that little man in black there, he say women can't have as much rights as men, 'cause Christ wasn't a woman! Where did your Christ come from! Where did your Christ come from? From God and a woman! Man had nothin' to do with Him.

If the first woman God ever made was strong enough to turn the world upside down all alone, these women together ought to be able to turn it back, and get it right side up again! And now they is askin' to do it, the men better let 'em.

Obliged to you for hearin' on me, and now ole Sojourner hasn't got nothin' more to say.

We women on this eve of the twenty-first century still have much to say. Our message is simple. It is, "America, finish the job—the job of granting freedom and equality to everybody in every sector of human interaction and involvement." We expect to see women in every place their competence suggests. "For Men Only" is not the American way.

Women and the Constitution: The Challenge

What is the challenge inherent in the subject "Women and the Constitution" 200 years after the delegates to the Constitutional Convention signed off on the document? I assume that question is included in the phrase, "A Bicentennial Perspective," which is a part of the subject of this symposium. We continue to celebrate the completion of the Constitution and honor and revere the signatories. We remain awed by the quality of mind shown by the Founding Fathers. We recite the Preamble and with a haughtiness of spirit laud over others that our fundamental law, the Constitution, was structured by us. We are proud that we, each and every one of us, are the "We the People" who ordained and established the Constitution of the United States of America. That is, we created the government and it exists to serve us. That is our faith.

As grand as all of that sounds, we know immediately it is not quite the whole truth. Women were not included in the Constitution. Women could not rightly claim to have been a part of the grand, sweeping "We the People." Why not? The rights and privileges of citizenship in the new country did not extend to women. They could not vote, hold public office, serve on a jury, tend bar, own property, study law, and one could go on. One may ask whether the founders were mean-spirited and just didn't like women. The answer is no. They loved women but had a very limited eighteenth-century notion about their role in the world.

John Adams, the second President of the United States, was not a delegate to the Constitutional Convention because in 1787 he was in London as our minister. He was, however, a member of the Continental Congress. Correspondence to him there from his wife, Abigail Adams, informs us of the desire of some women of that period to be included in the affairs of state. In 1776, Mrs. Adams urged her husband and the Founding Fathers of the new republic of the United States:

> In the new code of laws which I suppose it will be necessary for you to make, I desire you would remember the ladies and be more generous and favorable to them than your ancestors. Do not put such unlimited power into the hands of husbands. Remember, all men would be tyrants if they could. If particular care and attention is not paid to the ladies, we are determined to foment a rebellion, and will not hold ourselves bound by any laws in which we have no voice or representation.

That was a strong expression of desire, but history does not record an equivalent response. There does appear to have been a genuine feeling on the part of some men in power that women were weak and needed protection. The language of some of the early Supreme Court cases is revelatory and anachronistic. In *Bradwell v. Illinois* (1872), the Court upheld the right of a state to deny women the right to practice law. Justice Bradley:

> The natural and proper timidity and delicacy which belongs to the female sex evidently unfits it for many of the occupations of civil life. The constitution of family organization, which is founded in the divine ordinance, as well as in the nature of things, indicates the domestic sphere as that which properly belongs to the domain and functions of womanhood. . . . The paramount destiny and mission of women are to fulfill the noble and benign offices of wife and mother. This is the law of the Creator.

That feeling about the role of women was (should I say is?) very widespread and the voices of women in opposition muted.

This view regarding the place of women in American life was and is historical, social, cultural, natural, and seemed to conform to the universal fitness of things. It was this kind of long-lasting view which is in part responsible for the exclusion of women from the text of the Constitution. (I am aware that an argument can be made that women are included in Section 2 of Article IV, which states that "the citizens of each state shall be entitled to all privileges and immunities of citizens in the several states." I do not and would not make that argument. Such reasoning is tortured, at best. I make the same statement about the Fourth Amendment and its due process provision.)

This exclusion of women from the Constitution is no longer the case, but this changed status had a long, slow, and difficult period of development. The problem centered around the ambiguities implicit and explicit in the word *equality.* Equality is one of the foundation values of America. Our Declaration of Independence resounds with an egalitarian rhetoric. For years and generations, we appeared oblivious to our hypocrisy.

We had to shift our focus from *equal* meaning "same or similar" to equal as a modifier of rights, status, and opportunity. Men and women are not the same. Sylvia A. Law, a law professor, has written a superb article in *The University of Pennsylvania Law Review* titled "Rethinking Sex and the Constitution." In it she states,

> The reality of sex-based physical differences poses a significant problem for a society committed to ideals of individual human freedom and equality of opportunity. . . . To the extent that constitutional doctrine shapes culture and individual identity, an equality doctrine that denies the reality of biological difference in relation to reproduction reflects an idea about personhood that is inconsistent with people's actual experience of themselves and the world. . . . The central biological difference between men and women is that only women have the capacity to create a human being. . . . The power to create people is awesome. Men are profoundly disadvantaged by the reality that only women can produce a human being and experience the growth of a child in pregnancy.

This author then points out that society has more than made up for this profound disadvantage in providing men with extraordinary advantage— material and spiritual.

In 1868 the Fourteenth Amendment was added to the Constitution of the United States. The Civil War was over and the government was trying to sort out its obligations to its Black citizens. That amendment, among other things, guaranteed to all persons in this country "the equal protection of the laws"— that is, all persons except women. It was not until 1971 that the Supreme Court decided that women are included in the equal protection clause. To this date, we, women, are challenged to make sure that our rights are not ignored and that our participation in the life of the country is complete.

Joel Grossman and Richard Wells in their book *Constitutional Law and Judicial Policy Making* make the observation that

> There have been four interrelated strategies to bring about change in the rights of women. First, there have been political efforts to repeal offending state and federal laws. Second, there have been efforts to use the enforcement machinery of state and federal civil rights commissions. Third, efforts have been directed at Constitutional change. . . . Fourth . . . there have been continuing efforts to pass federal and state equal rights amendments.

All four strategies are needed and more. When the Equal Rights Amendment first passed, support in the House and Senate was overwhelming. It passed the House by a vote of 354–24 in October 1971 and the Senate in March 1972, by a vote of 84–8. It appeared to be moving toward early ratification. I was a member of the Texas Senate at that time, and all of our state leaders wanted Texas to be first to ratify. The Lieutenant Governor, the presiding officer of the Senate, came to me on the Senate floor and said that as soon as the amendment arrived, he would halt all business and recognize me to move for ratification. That is exactly what happened. (I don't think we were the first state to ratify in spite of our efforts.) The movement to ratify ERA stalled at thirty-five states. Momentum stopped. Opposition settled in. Revival? Problematical. All women do not support the Equal Rights Amendment. Those who do must respect the right of others to choose not to support ERA. Freedom of choice is not to be restricted to only those with whom we agree.

The language of the amendment is simple. "Equality of rights under the law shall not be denied or abridged by the United States or by any state on account of sex." That amendment, added to the Constitution, would end ambiguity and obfuscation and place women squarely within the letter of the Constitution. I give no odds on that occurring. But I do give great odds on the future, a future which has as its centerpiece men and women working together—in our common humanity—trying to ensure at every turn that we live in peace and freedom, with order and civility.

I conclude with a quote from a great First Lady, Eleanor Roosevelt. She said this at the UN General Assembly in 1952:

> I believe we will have better government in our countries when men and women discuss public issues together and make their decisions on the basis of their differing areas of experience and their common concern for the welfare of their families and their world. . . . Too often the great decisions are originated and given form in bodies made up wholly of men, or so completely dominated by them that whatever of special value women have to offer is shunted aside without expression.

That must not be. Our task is too great. Our hold on the future, too tenuous. Our relationships, too fragile. Time remaining, too short. Space we occupy, too small. Life too great—to hang out a sign—For Men Only.

Government and Democracy

One of the earliest speeches we have on record in the Jordan Archives is a speech delivered by Barbara Jordan in 1967 at her alma mater, Texas Southern University, as a Law Day speech. She was then State Senator representing the Eleventh District in Houston, Texas. Her convictions on ethics, ideals of the Constitution, opinions on the responsibility of government, and principles of life are all encapsulated in this first explosive speech titled "The Law, the Promise, and the Power."

The other speeches in this section all explicate Jordan's philosophy on government and the people: "In Search of Humanity," "Civil Liberties: Inoperative? Inaudible? Unintelligible? Expletive Deleted?," "Can We Govern Ourselves?," "Harvard University Commencement Address," and "Council on Foundations Keynote Address."

The stakes are too high for government to be a spectator sport.

Harvard University Commencement Address
JUNE 16, 1977

Law Day Speech
Texas Southern University
Houston, Texas
APRIL 27, 1967

The Law, the Promise, and the Power

Etched across the face of the United States Supreme Court Building are these words: "Equality before the Law." The symbol of justice wears a blindfold in a groping effort to guarantee its fairness and rightness. The prince and the pauper are brought before the bar. Do they experience equal treatment? Are the words "Equality before the Law" just a maxim, a pronouncement, a truth, a fact, or a promise?

No nation-state has excelled America in the nobility of her pronouncements. The time-honored words of the Declaration of Independence continue to excite and inspire the spirit of this country. The Preamble to the United States Constitution is painstakingly memorized by little children with hesitant tongues. The great Civil War Amendments, the Thirteenth, Fourteenth, and Fifteenth, are made the subject of a special section in American history courses. The solemn pledge of allegiance, ". . . one nation, under God, indivisible, with liberty and justice for all," pales into rhetoric with repetition. Freedom and equality become a part of the "ism" of America, for history tells us that it is for these principles that a revolution was fought and won. The words were always there and they still are. Yet, we continue to struggle for their meaning. We are still trying to define America, to affirm and actualize its promise.

This process of definition, affirmation, and actualization is not easy. The restlessness of the youth who belong to this moment of history presents stark evidence of this difficulty. It has a human concern as it fulfills its function to secure justice, protect the citizenry, punish the lawless, preserve the peace, and guarantee to every man the right not to have his manhood violated and his basic personality or humanity dehumanized. The power and compulsion inherent in the law makes the fulfillment of its functions possible.

A noted jurist, Judge Learned Hand, once said,

The law must have an authority supreme over the will of the individual; thus the law surpasses the deliverances of even the most exalted of its prophets; the momentum of its will alone makes it effective to coerce the individual and reconciles him to his subserviency. The Pious Traditionalism of the law has its roots in a sound conviction of this necessity; it must be content to lay behind the best inspiration of its time until it feels behind the weight of such general acceptance as will give sanction to its pretension to unquestioned dictation. Yet, with this piety must go a taste for courageous experiment, by which alone the law has been built as we have it an indubitable structure, organic and living.

We could at length question Judge Hand's initial statement concerning the supremacy of the law over the *will* of the individual. If by *will* he refers to the *power at the center* of every human being which shapes and determines his personality, individuality, or character, I could not agree that the law is supreme. If by *will* he refers to the individual's tendency or inclination or willingness to deviate and refuse to conform to given social structures, we may find an area of agreement.

We are concerned in Judge Hand's statement with his view of the Pious Traditionalism and the law and its taste for courageous experiment. At times, the two are in conflict. There is a familiar example of this conflict.

The doctrine of "Separate but Equal" became a part of the "Pious Tradition of the Law" in 1890, in the *Plessy v. Ferguson* decision. In the School Desegregation Decision of 1954, the U.S. Supreme Court decided to experiment with its abolition. The experiment was not very courageous, for the mandate of "all deliberate speed" gave Southern jurists an escape hatch. Ten years later the courts and the Department of Justice decided that it was finally time for the exercise of courage. The time for all deliberate speed is at an end. Did they say now? The transition from tradition to courageous experiment in the law, in this instance, took almost ninety years. The law does have an underlying human concern, but its concern must sometimes wait for the weight of general acceptance and sanction. That weight is at times *very slow* in being applied.

The Civil Rights Act of 1964 was indeed the work of a courageous Congress. The Congress of the United States, through that bill, made illegal the exclusion of persons from that promise we referred to earlier, if that exclusion was based on race, color, sex, or national origin. Is it right that we commend our national lawmakers for their courage in this regard? Is the Civil Rights Act an example of the dynamics of the organic, living law? Or is that act a result of the actualization of the power of a people? I prefer to agree with the latter. There is a persistent tension between the conservative, pious traditionalism of the law and its taste for courageous experiment, and sometimes the people are caught between these two forces. However, because of its underlying human concern, it can and does respond to the pressure and power of a people if that power is valid, real, actualized.

We have now referred to power in a kind of dual sense: the power inherent in the law to compel, coerce, and enforce; and the power in a people which, when actualized, causes the law to respond. (I hasten to add that the law is not the only structure which responds to this power.)

Paul Tillich, in writing on love, power, and justice, had this to say about power. "The power of being becomes manifest only in the process in which it actualizes its power. Power is real only in its actualization, in the encounter with the other bearers of power and in the everchanging balance which is the result of these encounters. . . . Power is the possibility of overcoming non-being."

The struggle of the Negro could be described as a valiant effort to overcome and destroy the last vestige of his "non-being"—his invisibility—and an accompanying effort to secure his individuality, his wholeness, and [his] relevance as a human being. As long as the Negro remained a thing apart, an object to be dealt with and cared for, there was no need for legal or ruling structures to act on his behalf. He was certainly nonthreatening, for, judging the concern of the "power structure," the Negro really wasn't there. He was not "in-being." Had the Negro been content to remain invisible, this present encounter between bearers of power—sometimes called the Negro Revolt—would never have occurred. But, fortunately, he did not choose to remain content, or history did not choose to allow him to bask in his external *docility*, or maybe it was politics, or perhaps [it was] a creative choice. In any event, the possibility of power was there. The people always had the possibility of the exercise of power. It was not latent or dormant. It was there; it was moving; it was vibrant. For, to be power at all, it has to be real. Not a bare threat—not emotional tumult and shouting—but power in fact. So, this power of a people worked through to the surface and gradually began to manifest itself as dynamic power through massive action, direct and nonviolent. The power of a suppressed minority encountered the power of the ruling group, and the result was a slight change in balance. This must not be interpreted as an assertion that the ruling group or the "power structure" changed its components. It did not. The weight shifted; the balance changed; power became less than total; a check was introduced.

This change in balance has been accompanied by conflict. The conflict at times has been open and physical. It has occurred across bargaining tables, in legislative chambers, and in the streets. Charles Silberman, member of the editorial board of *Fortune* magazine and author of the provocative book *Crisis in Black and White*, said at a recent convention of NAIRO, "Conflict is inevitable. Power cannot be achieved without it. Power cannot be acquired without conflict. For no group ever surrenders power voluntarily. Nor can power be received as a gift; it must be taken, for it is in the process of striving for power that people become powerful. It is in the process of fighting for freedom that they become free." The recognition of the possibility of power, followed by the striving, which is followed by "becoming," completes the cycle.

The law intervened in an effort to reduce the conflict occasioned by the encounter of powers. One might argue that the law did not intervene as an impartial arbiter, but that it intervened on the side of the striving minority. This position could not, however, be successfully argued. The principles of equality and justice have always and historically been a part of the tradition of the law. They are basic, fundamental, and inherent in the rule of law. Our American heritage presupposes a government of law before which all men stand as equals. Our judicial pronouncements indicate a respect for justice under law and the necessity of the concept in our social order. Mr. Justice Cardoza, in the famous case of *Palko v. Connecticut*, established the test for determining presence or absence of due process of law in the question, "Does the action complained of violate those fundamental principles of liberty and justice which lie at the base of all of our civil and political institutions?" If the answer is yes, this constitutes a denial of due process. If the answer is no, there has been no denial of due process, the key words in the determination of *liberty* and *justice*. Therefore, when the law intervenes on the side of the striving minority, it is not showing partiality but is simply fulfilling its historical function.

The question which can appropriately be raised in this discussion is whether or not justice is always a component of law. *If* justice is inherent in enacted laws, why is injustice at times the result of the enactment and enforcement of laws? Resulting injustice is not the consequence of law but the consequence of the actions of a ruling group which has no sense of justice or liberty. Unjust laws, most typical of the South, evidence this. The tenets of justice cannot be drafted, compiled, or reproduced. They cannot be reduced to IBM cards and processed in an electronic computer producing a result of mathematical accuracy. There is no automatic application of principles which would guarantee that justice is done. Each case and each cause must be considered on its own particular circumstances.

There are certain principles of justice that provide guidelines for the administration of justice. Tillich calls these principles adequacy, equality, freedom, and liberty. Adequacy here refers to the need for a present, relevant, timely justice. There is an active tendency on the part of man to preserve and conserve that form which has best served his aims, aspirations, and selfhood. He is reluctant, and at times unwilling, to go or act beyond that which is part of his experience, whether it is adequate or not. He wants to continue in the shelter of past custom and tradition and is willing to risk their continuation beyond the point of their adequacy. Such continuation often results in injustice. Our current racial troubles provide sufficient evidence of this. The struggle, particularly of the South, may be described as an effort to maintain custom and tradition, which is legalized, codified, and statutory. The continuation of the old will continue to perpetuate injustice. Tillich's principle of adequacy must also be applied to this rigidity and resistance of the South.

The second principle, equality, refers to the indiscriminate treatment of all persons as persons. This equality must be implicit in every law if justice is to be realized. The "freedom" of justice must release every person to be himself. It is not freedom to transgress but freedom to be. The principle of liberty is seen as that form of freedom which removes restraining barriers which would enslave if allowed to continue.

The foregoing principles are a part of justice, and justice is a part of the historic traditionalism of the law. All are not always present in all laws, but the absence of one results in injustice.

The administration of justice is a recognized and legitimate function of all states, nation-states. Every state has a justicial arm. The direction and method of administration may differ according to the politics of the state, but the function remains.

We use here the terminology *nation-state* because it most clearly expresses the collective order that we will now view. The terms *state* and *nation* are frequently used interchangeably. The term *nation*, strictly speaking as evidenced by its etymology (nascii—to be born), indicates relation of birth or origin and implies a common race, usually characterized by community of language and customs. The term *state*—a more specific term—connotes, in the international sense, a people permanently occupying a fixed territory, bound together by common laws and customs into a body politic, possessing an organized government, and capable of conducting relations with other states. The term thus refers to an organization or institution-relation between people.

The state, with its organized government, has been made the target of criticism by persons who have been unable personally to relate to the state. It has been abused as an evil structure bent on limiting personal freedoms. Its critics can see it only as a thing requiring obedience and subserviency. The state has been viewed as having an objective reality but no subjective existence. These views are the result of misunderstanding and inaccurate interpretation of the true nature, character, and function of the state. The state *is* people and exists for people. It has no function that is not people related. It is people, ordered and structured in a composite whole for the protection of people, the maintenance of order in the society, and the conduct of relations with other organized people. Therefore, one cannot separate a state from its people for it is its people—organized or institutionalized. The result of this organization is the entity we call the state. The state cannot speak for itself and all people cannot speak for the state. Therefore, we of the state designate those who will have the authority to speak for the state. We acknowledge them as spokesmen. Whenever the chosen spokesmen fail to express in word and deed the best interest of the people, the people may withdraw their acknowledgment and choose new spokesmen. This designation and/or withdrawal should express the will of the majority of the people. But the majority rarely expresses its choice, not because it cannot but because it will not. (The reasons for this are the subject matter of another speech.) We will simply say here that the majority both does not care and cannot see how its expression can make any real difference. The special interests in the state do not have to control the state. There is no compulsion, legal or moral, which requires the acquiescence of the people to the control of the special interest groups.

We have said that the administration of justice is a recognized and legitimate function of all nation-states. This administration takes the form of the enactment of laws and the enforcement of compliance. Can we rely on the tradition of the rule of law and enforcement of the written statutes to secure justice for the people? I submit that we cannot, for the jurist must bring to bear upon the written word and administrative process a sense of ethics and morality if justice is to be made secure. Chief Justice Earl Warren of the United States Supreme Court, in a speech to the Jewish Theological Seminary of America, stated,

> The inability of man-made laws to deal with the ethical questions of society and therefore the need of men to seek spiritual guidance is basic. [Man-made law fails to provide us with answers regarding our moral duty.] Society would come to grief without ethics. If there were no sense of love in families, if there were no sense of loyalty, if friendship meant nothing, if we all or any large proportion of us were motivated by avarice and greed, society would collapse almost as completely as though it lacked law. Law in a civilized society presupposes ethical commitment. It presupposes the existence of a broad area of human conduct controlled only by ethical norms and not subject to law at all.

In Search of Humanity

When politicians admit their mortality and our relative mutual dependency, we can expect humane government to exist in America—a government which cares about the well-being of the governed. The Founding Fathers of America were ordinary men—British men who could barely tolerate the notion of separatism from Great Britain. Acts committed by the Crown against the colonies were so outrageous and so against the order of nature and men that these citizens of British America were compelled to sever the ties to family, to parents, to mother country, to the British Empire. These were scared men sacrificing their heritage and their history to begin what then was an unfathomable experiment in government of, by, and for the people. Their ideas and their sacrifices defy quantification. They were great and enormous. No man at Philadelphia 200 years ago could have realized the depth and breadth and impact of their collective dream for America. Nor could we, two years ago, have fathomed the depth of depravity in our government that is the antithesis of the ideals to which those men committed their lives.

Thomas Jefferson, at the time of the First Continental Congress, gave the simplest formula for good government. It may have been forgotten by the Nixon administration. It is logical, simple, and true. The public official who is a moral man knows it instinctively. He does not need a chief of staff or domestic counselor to furnish an explanation abstract of the formula for him.

Jefferson wrote: "The whole art of government consists in the art of being honest."

Pursuit of a policy of honesty by our leaders in government may regain the people's loss of confidence and restore diminished credibility. A return to the great principles of right and wrong might allay some of the suffering and violence in the world. Our officials must recognize that it is wrong for us to

39

harbor sick and poor people in this land of wealth; that it is wrong to tolerate racial hatred and injustice heaped upon injustice for everyone who is not white, male, and forty; that it is not right for this scourge of inflation to decay every fiber in the fabric of our society.

How soon will this cloth we wear rend apart and leave us naked before this world? Already the world economy is nearing collapse—Italy's government has just fallen for the thirty-sixth time since World War II; the governments of Portugal, Greece, Cyprus, and Chile have changed hands in sometimes bloody upheaval. In America, we exorcised ourselves of a President who failed to remember that "Kings (Presidents) are the servants, not the proprietors of the people."

In our country, inflation is over 11.2 percent, unemployment has reached 5.8 percent, and in August food prices soared—giving us now a 46.8 percent yearly inflation on food. Inflation has dwarfed other world problems and neither micro or macro economists [nor] democratic or republican politicians can enter this maze without getting burned. We need leaders willing to take the risks of leadership so that our weakest citizens are not consumed, so that our country is not consumed. No one has as yet been willing to take the real risks to quench with finality the fires of inflation. More is required of our leaders in government than sloganism, traditionalism, piety, and conventionalism. We need people in public office with the strength to do what is both difficult and right.

We have drunk the last of the wine, yet this Republican administration seems to think we can produce a new vintage by stomping over the same old grapes. If the past is prologue, we should know that the anti-inflation policies of the past offer no hope for present and future lasting solutions.

When will we be willing to put human suffering ahead of self-interest? When will the burden of the private person lead to political instability, not just economic instability? Our priorities must shift if the American birthday is to be a celebration of a two-century-old adolescent among nations and not a wake for a dead, moribund experiment.

The human condition *must* be improved and government *must* help to improve it. Government is not here just to build roads and bridges, defend our shores, control our money, and raise lofty marble monuments to past glories. Government, by our participation and support of it, is our appointed mediator, prosecutor, defender—our means of guaranteeing our freedoms and protecting our frailties. It is people, not things, that make this country great. It is the capacity for human kindness and compassion that gives depth and meaning to life in America. The men and women who gave birth to this country had a dream. They had a dream of freedom, of happiness, of life lived with purpose and pride, of justice and peace through law. We can begin to recommit ourselves to the well-being of every citizen in this country. We need men and women in the government of this country who can bring substance and substantive content, creativity and innovation, caring and compassion to this country's style and to this country's rhetoric. Those men in Philadelphia were not writing great speeches for history when they spoke of love, peace, loyalty, truth, honesty, rights, compassion, humanity, and humaneness—they were speaking from their troubled hearts—that is what made them great.

Those men were sacrificing their lives and their fortunes—when will we be willing to put human suffering ahead of self-interest? At the recent Presidential Economic Summit, a priest, one of the participants, had sat listening to the two days of debate. In the final question-and-answer period, he stood and addressed his question to all of the participants: "Who was willing to make the sacrifices that had to be made for everyone to survive?" No one had been willing to think about the welfare of someone else or the necessity of self-sacrifice. How can inflation be stopped when self-interest is the rule of the day?

It is our task to impress upon our leaders that people are the stuff of America, that simple human dignity is more important than tax-free bonds or exempt dividends on preferred stock. Compassion for the sick, the poor, the elderly is not anathema to the efficient functioning of a democratic government. Honesty in the dealings of public men is a right every citizen must demand. Public men and women make the decisions in government, and private men and women can take away their right to decide.

Only when men and women in government are accountable to the citizenry, accountable to morality, accountable to the Constitution, will inflation, disruption, and discontent be solved and the spirit restored.

The republic has weathered a constitutional storm and our institutions have survived. Can we weather the economic, social, and political storms ahead? Only when men and women are elected to public office—who believe that it is the business of government to "promote the general welfare"—will there be hope of reforming our tax laws, reforming our social security system, reforming our health care delivery system, and reforming the business of politics. I hope that somehow we can return a sense of security and pride and belonging to this country and develop solutions that will inure to the benefit of all of us. I want us to become great again, to feel great again.

The world looks to us as the leader of the free world to restore sanity to the conduct of the people of the world. The house of America must be put in order. Our friends will judge us by our conduct and seek guidelines for their own behavior. The earth is too small, in too much turmoil, for us to do otherwise. I would like to read a few lines written by Robert Frost in 1916.

> I'd like to get away from earth awhile
> And then come back to it and begin over
> May no fate willfully misunderstand me
> And half grant what I wish and snatch me away

> Not to return. Earth's the right place for love;
> I don't know where it's likely to go better.

I don't know where it's more likely to get better than in America, if we bring love and compassion and understanding back into our lives and the life of our country. I disagree with Mr. Frost though—I don't want to leave and neither does Adlai Stevenson. We believe that human values are worth fighting for. Good government begins with good people willing to change, to fight, and to defend our government. To preserve that [which is] worthy of preserving and to discard that which is unworthy. The wounds in the body politic can be administered to only by men and women of good conscience—people who care about America, its heritage, its greatness, its people.

I am a patriot. I believe that the world community does better when America leads from a position of strength and confidence. I believe that the people of America live better when Democrats sit in the seats of power. . . . We are not frightened by big government. We use it as the paramount instrumentality to get things done for people.

On November 5, the people of America must send a message to Washington. The message should begin, "To the President and the Members of the Congress of the United States: We recognize that you are moral and ordinary men and women. However, we, the people of the United States, have entrusted to you our freedoms. Take care of them. We expect you to be honest in all you do. Tell the truth. Don't lie. Do justly. Be fair. Know the difference between right and wrong, and do what is right. Settle your disputes peacefully. Adhere to the law as the great citizen-protector. Do this, Mr. President—Ladies and Gentlemen of the Congress, and a monument will be erected to you which no room can contain.

"Thank you. Your friend, the American public."

Civil Liberties: Inoperative? Inaudible? Unintelligible? Expletive Deleted?

On April 30, a document was submitted to the Committee on the Judiciary of the House of Representatives which purported to be recorded conversations of President Nixon. There were omissions. One thousand six hundred seventy portions of conversations were said to be "inaudible" or "unintelligible." One wonders what act or deed remains undiscovered because it cannot be heard or understood.

Is it possible that the vitiation of individual freedoms, of civil liberties, is masked by such words?

Civil liberties: Inoperative? Inaudible? Unintelligible? ... Expletive deleted? An affirmative answer to those questions appears justified when we view past and present events.

The government has admitted that it wiretapped its own employees—and that some of these taps continued after the employees left the government—and that it wiretapped newsmen. The government has admitted to seventeen taps. Newsmen, fearful that the First Amendment protection of the Constitution is more rhetoric than fact, seek a Newsmen's Shield Law. The politicization of the FBI becomes the subject matter of congressional oversight. The President's right to suspend the Fourth Amendment guarantee against "unreasonable searches and seizures" in the interest of "national security" is defended. The concept of "executive privilege" has been used cavalierly to disguise gross intrusions into the private life of the individual.

You, the graduate, emerge from academia with the expectation or hope that you will be free to fulfill your life as you define it. You have a basis to

43

presume that the government will not interfere with your pursuit. That presumption is based on what is known and understood about the history of freedom and liberty in America. That history began in 1776. But in the almost 200 years which have passed since that date, the freedoms so painfully gained have been constantly threatened by erosion. That threat has become so serious that one can ask the serious question of whether "civil liberties" is any longer an operative ideal of the United States.

Thomas Jefferson in his first inaugural address on March 4, 1801, reminded the American people of the principles for which the Revolutionary War had been fought:

> Equal and exact justice to all men, of whatever state or persuasion, religious or political; peace, commerce, and honest friendship with all nations, entangling alliances with none. . . . Freedom of religion, freedom of the press, freedom of person under the protection of the *habeas corpus*, and trial by juries impartially selected. These principles form the bright constellation which has gone before us, and guided our steps through an age of revolution and reformation. The wisdom of our sages and the blood of our heroes have been devoted to their attainment. They should be the creed of our political faith, the text of civil instruction, the touchstone by which to try the services of those we trust; and should we wander from them in moments of error or alarm, let us hasten to retrace our steps and to regain the road which alone leads to peace, liberty, and safety.

Jefferson went on to ask a question that is strikingly relevant for Americans today: "Would the honest patriot, in the full tide of successful experiment, abandon a government which has so far kept us free and firm, on the theoretic and visionary fear that his government, the world's best hope, may by possibility want energy to preserve itself?"

It is the stuff of America that its citizens be free of government's intrusions into their private and personal affairs. That concept of freedom is firmly etched in our Constitution and Bill of Rights. There are no gaps or inexplicable hums in that document. The language flows well. The thirty-nine men who signed the Constitution of the United States fought for its ratification because they knew they had to build a new concept of a nation, the touchstone of which would be liberty, freedom, and justice. The doctrine of separation of powers and the structure of checks and balances became the themes for ratification. This government was so formed to provide maximum protection of the people from gross abuse of power by officials and governmental excesses of power. The signers of the Constitution believed they had constructed a government which would "secure the blessings of liberty to ourselves and our posterity."

Over twenty years ago, writing about "The Crisis in Freedom" in the June 1952 issue of *The Progressive*, Dr. Alexander Meiklejohn stated the compelling argument for the need to strengthen individual independence and freedom of thought and expression in any conflict with the power of government authority:

Freedom of belief and of expression is not hostile to security. We need not choose between them. On the contrary, freedom, as a mode of life, as a form of government, is far more efficient, far more dependable in time of danger, than any form of suppression. It is, in fact, the only governing form which, in a world of rapid social change, gives promise of permanence and stability. If we keep faith with it, nothing human can destroy it. As we lose faith in it, we are destroying it.

In modern technological nations, however, individual and personal rights are increasingly threatened by the often conflicting demands of the state for expediency, efficiency, and stability. While the capability for secretly invading the private affairs of individual citizens has been vastly increased by improved technology and sophisticated electronics, the legal mechanisms to administer appropriate public controls over the exercise of these powers by agencies of the government have failed to keep pace with events.

As Jefferson warned so prophetically, "The natural progress of things is for liberty to yield and government to gain ground." In recent years, we have witnessed a willingness to accelerate the erosion of those guiding principles which have been the genius of America. And this erosion has been all the more insidious because it has happened one step at a time; because it has been perpetrated by those who enjoy the unsuspecting trust of a great people for the highest offices of the land; and because it has been masked in the disguise of emergency—the need to maintain "law and order," to protect "national security," and so on.

We know that an American President and his top assistants believed that they could suspend the First and Fourth Amendments in the Bill of Rights when they perceived a threat to the national security. We know that there have been attempts to use the instruments of government against political opponents and other citizens exercising their rights of free speech.

The Constitution and the Bill of Rights established an important and delicate balance between the government's interests and the interests of the governed. It dictates the need for the explicit civil liberty and political freedom of each citizen, as well as the security and welfare of the entire society. Today, this equilibrium is in question.

The history of individual liberty, and particularly the right of privacy, has been a history of resistance to governmental encroachments and an insistence upon fair procedural protections. Where liberty has prevailed, the rights of man have been translated into action; where liberty has lost, only silence has followed the dying echoes of declarations of freedom.

For example, unannounced entry into private homes was denounced in English common law as early as 1603. In a classic case, it was declared that

> In all cases where the King is party, the sheriff (if the doors be not open) may break in the party's house, either to arrest him, or to do other execution

of the King's process, if otherwise he cannot enter. But, before he breaks it, he ought to signify the cause of his coming, and to make request to open doors. . . .

In 1766, the sanctity of the individual's right of privacy in his home and the importance of protecting against unlawful invasion of privacy by the government were again argued with magnificent eloquence. The British were having difficulty collecting an excise tax that the Parliament had imposed upon cider. To solve their problem, it was proposed that the tax collectors be given the authority to enforce their cider tax by entering a man's house without knocking. When this proposal was debated in the House of Lords, William Pitt closed his argument in opposition to this government invasion of privacy by stating:

> The poorest man may, in his cottage, bid defiance to all the forces of the Crown. It may be frail. Its roof may shake. The wind may blow through it. The storm may enter. The rain may enter. But the King of England cannot enter. All his force dares not cross the threshold of that ruled tenement.

Two hundred and eight years after Pitt's stirring affirmation of individual privacy and resistance to the invasion of the homes by forces of the Crown, it is again necessary to argue the case against the government's trampling of personal rights with equal factor. In 1766, the British tax collector sought authority to break into a private home to collect a cider tax; in 1973, agents of federal, state, and local governments in the United States acted on uncorroborated tips and without warrants, and proceeded to batter down the doors of two Collinsville, Illinois, homes and terrorize two law-abiding families in their mistaken frenzy.

Last summer, John Ehrlichman testified before the Senate Watergate Committee. Senator Herman Talmadge, a member of that committee, asked him about the principle, derived from English law, that not even a king can enter a man's cottage without his consent. Ehrlichman replied, "I am afraid that has been considerably *eroded* over the years." Eroded, inoperative, inaudible, unintelligible, expletive deleted.

In addition to the continuing reality of smashed doors and actual physical invasions of private homes, government forces have a more insidious tool: electronic eyes and ears that need break no doors to silently steal privileged thoughts and record private deeds.

This administration's claim of an inherent right to conduct surveillance, to wiretap, to break and enter private homes without a warrant and without knocking, and without any recourse to due process of law, on the grounds of national security, control of organized crime, and other reasons, has opened the door to governmental lawlessness on a massive scale.

At least fifty different federal agencies have substantial investigative and enforcement functions, providing a corps of more than 20,000 "investigators" working for agencies such as the FBI, Naval Intelligence, the Post Office, the Narcotics Bureau of the Justice Department, the Securities and Exchange Commission, the Internal Revenue Service, the Food and Drug Administration, the State Department, the Civil Service Commission, and even the Department of Agriculture.

The events of the past several years in particular have revealed a shocking pattern of disregard for constitutional principles of law and due process in the highest offices and agencies of the government. It is apparent that the powerful tools of government spying and espionage against private citizens in pursuit of their lawful activities have not been kept within legitimate boundaries through self-restraint or self-discipline. Declarations of *high* moral purpose have been used to elevate *low* deeds, and the distinctions between the proper goals of government actions and the improper means by which they are prosecuted have become blurred.

No one has stated the case against governmental lawlessness more eloquently than Justice Louis Brandeis in a strongly worded dissent in the 1928 case of Olmstead against the United States:

> In a government of laws, existence of the government will be imperiled if it fails to observe the law scrupulously. Our government is the potent, the omnipresent teacher. For good or ill, it teaches the whole people by its example. Crime is contagious. If the government becomes the lawbreaker, it breeds contempt for law; it invites man to become a law unto himself; it invites anarchy. To declare that in the administration of the criminal law the end justifies the means—to declare that the government may commit crimes in order to secure the conviction of a private criminal—would bring terrible retribution.

If one thing is clear about the erosion of civil liberties, it is that there is no clear line between freedom and repression. Freedom is a fluid, intangible condition of our society. It thrives at some periods and is beset at others. It is lost not all at once, but by degrees.

The events of the past few years have not produced a repressive society, but they have resulted in an atmosphere in which freedom is on the defensive. For perhaps the first time in our history, there is room for the belief that tyranny in America is possible.

If faith in a future which revives the good in our history is to be restored, you must restore it. What has been lost can be regained if you have the energy to regain it. It may now appear that America is adrift—that the winds are not favorable for the ship of state. The words of Seneca are applicable: "If a man does not know to what port he is sailing, no wind is favorable." You cannot afford the laziness of the drifter. You must know to what port you sail, for the confidence and sureness of your knowledge may help nudge this country in the right direction.

Daniel Webster once said:

> Let us develop the resources of our land, call forth its powers, build up its institutions, promote all its great interests, and see whether we also in our day and generation may not perform something worthy to be remembered.

Civil liberties: Inoperative? Inaudible? Unintelligible? Expletive deleted?

Answer those questions in the negative. Affirm that "civil liberties" is operative, audible, intelligible, and that no expletive is necessary. Affirm that and you will have performed something worthy to be remembered.

Association of American Railroads
Tuscon, Arizona
OCTOBER 19, 1994

Can We Govern Ourselves?

That may sound like a strange question coming from someone who has been directly or indirectly connected to government for the past thirty years. It really is a presently vital question in the face of the erratic cycle of cynicism and optimism reflected in the attitudes of the American people. We seem to swing from manic highs to inexplicable lows within the shortest period of time. The pages of newspapers all across the country show an almost moment-to-moment measure of public mood swings by pollsters and pundits. Each major candidate for public office has his or her in-house pollsters instantly ready to communicate the latest positive or negative reaction. Their presence seems to loom larger today than in other political seasons. Why?

The answers are not simple. There are some contributing factors which cannot be ignored. The depth and extent of cynicism today appears to be greater than most political observers can recall.

Conventional wisdom has been consistent in predicting that, notwithstanding the low esteem in which the public holds Congress, the people like their own Senator or Representative and will return him or her to office. The conclusion has been rendered inoperative for this approaching November 8 election. You have read of those icons of the Democratic Party who are threatened with defeat: Kennedy, Cuomo, Foley et al. If that happens, it will shake the very foundation of the party and could weaken liberalism as a viable political ideology.

How can one explain the depth of today's cynicism and the strong, almost palpable anti-incumbent feeling? The explanation rests with the people. There is a general feeling that nothing works, particularly government and its numer-

49

ous departments and divisions. The notion of unworkability is fed by the dissonance between what the people want and what they get. The Constitution of the United States promises to each state a "republican form of government." This is a guarantee found in Article 4, Section 4, of the fundamental law. That proviso ensures a heavy reliance on people input. A monarchy—one-person rule—cannot be a republic. An oligarchy—government by a few people—cannot be a republic. Only a democracy can be a republic, and the people have the exquisite burden of governing. The supreme power of governing is held by us.

Does that then mean that we are cynical about ourselves when we hold government in such low esteem? I believe that [cynicism] has to be a part of the answer, but only a part. As a democratic republic, we do not govern directly. We govern through our elected representatives, and we have known since 1776 that if our representatives fail in their execution of the functions of their office, it is our right—it is our duty—to withdraw the authority to govern and select someone else in their stead.

If predictions about this year are correct, there will be wholesale changes in the occupants of political office. That exercise is called "democracy in action" and is no cause for despair.

What I have just said is a kind of textbook explanation of government. What was not mentioned is those factors which could interfere with the free, undeterred choice of the people. A large quantity of money owned and used in [a candidate's] campaign can skew the playing field and make the race unfair. There are several races around about which that could be said. Such allegations have been made about contests in California, Texas, Florida, New York, and others. Is the role played by money illegal? No. We continue to tolerate as governors of ourselves the intrusive presence of money in politics.

Extreme partisanship can deny [to] those of weak will and conviction, thoughtful analysis and rational choice. In my opinion what we saw in the waking days of the 103rd Congress was partisanship at its worst. You know that I am a Democrat. But what I am about to say does not lay all of the blame for the failure of certain major policy initiatives at the feet of the Republican Party.

With the election of Bill Clinton, the Democrats had it all: the White House, the Senate, the House of Representatives. We lacked the discipline to govern. Both parties at times appeared to forget the first duty of the public official: to serve the public interest. That is not an easy or transitory requirement of public service. It asks that the officeholder deny self-interest at all times and place the general concerns of the public first. That requirement is in fact almost antithetical to human nature. We have all learned quite early in our lives the old saw, "self-preservation is the first law of nature." We never seriously tried to analyze such a statement but regarded it as a given without a thought. Who among you is willing to suppress his own interest out of a general concern first for the common good? We ask that of those who serve us as officeholders. If the elected official feels that is an unfair burden, the public need simply remind the official that he volunteered for the office. However, that is not the end of our responsibility as citizens. As citizens we are parties to the social contract which guides our actions as we daily interact with our fellow citizens. That agreement does not leave us free to roam the political landscape at will. All requirements are not on the side of the officeholder. There is a concomitant civic duty which each of us bears. It mandates that we become informed on the issues and express our view in public forums and indicate our decision at the ballot box on election day. That civic duty is no less important than the actions of the public official.

The bottom line was still best expressed by a young Benjamin Franklin; he said, "Here, sir, the people govern." And that is the whole matter.

This is the time for you to interfere and help the government regain its authority and restore the public trust. I'm counting on you.

Harvard University Commencement Address

Were I to begin by saying I was pleased to have been invited to speak to the Harvard community on this occasion, you might consider it nothing more than a trite beginning. If so, you would be in error. I have always held Harvard in high regard and viewed a Harvard education as the unexcelled badge of intellectual achievement, if not superiority. My appearance here may not honor you but it certainly honors me. One reason I attended Boston University Law School was so that I could be close.

My earliest brush with Harvard occurred over twenty years ago, when I was a junior at Texas Southern University. I might add that TSU, originally named Texas State University for Negroes, was created in order to keep Blacks out of the University of Texas. The Harvard debate team came to TSU. I was a debater. I didn't understand why representatives of this school so revered by me would come to debate TSU. My perplexity notwithstanding, the debate occurred. The judge's decision was that the debate ended in a tie. It now occurs to me that if Harvard students were as superior as everyone thought, they should have won. Since the score was tied, we must have won.

So before beginning my speech, I hereby declare that in a debate between Texas Southern University and Harvard University, Texas Southern won. If you have any surplus trophies around, I will take one home to the team. And if you should run into the Harvard debaters, Jared Diamond and James Sikes, offer them my condolence.

The invitation to be here today appeared designed either to challenge or intimidate. I quote an unedited paragraph from the letter of invitation. "We invite you to speak on whatever topic you find suitable. A number of Harvard commencement speeches have been memorable. Perhaps, the most memorable was that of Secretary of State George C. Marshall, who used the occasion to announce the Marshall plan for Europe."

A Jordan plan to create, ameliorate, or eliminate will not be announced at this time. If I think of one at anytime during the remainder of my life, I will request a return visit.

Even though I will not present a plan which will be celebrated thirty years hence, I will talk to you about a problem which concerns me greatly. The answers are not in the back of the book—nor at the end of the speech.

Of late, many articles have been written and speeches delivered about the importance of the input of the people into the affairs of government. Symbolic gestures have been staged and populist rhetoric has been translated into law. The point of it all is to make people feel that they really do count and that the government does care what they think. Such actions are said to be the logical extension and proper fulfillment of an amorphous something called "the promise of America."

Do the governors of America sincerely believe that people are a valuable resource of the government, or do the governors believe the people are an indispensable nuisance to a democracy?

Let us reflect on our history for a moment. The Declaration of Independence, a relatively short document, is rife with references to people. In the very first sentence of the Declaration:

When ... it becomes necessary for one *people* to dissolve the political bands ...

Whenever a government becomes destructive of certain unalienable rights ...

It is the right of the *people* to alter or abolish it.

In itemizing the oppressiveness of George III,

He has refused to pass other laws for the accommodation of large districts of *people*, unless those *people* would relinquish the right of representation in the legislature.
   ... His invasions on the rights of the *people*.
   ... He has sent hither swarms of officers to harass our *people*.
   ... He has destroyed the lives of our *people*.
   ... And finally, the declaration is made in the name and by authority of the good *people*.

Subsequently, the Constitution augmented and implemented the political philosophy espoused in the Declaration of Independence. The raison d'être of the new government—the political well-being of the people—and the government's source of authority—the people—was once more and again [its quintessence].

We the *people* of the United States.

The House of Representatives—chosen every second year by the *people*.

The right of the *people* peaceably to assemble.

The right of the *people* to be secure in their persons.

Enumeration of certain rights retained by the *people*. Certain powers reserved to the *people*.

As the states proceeded to ratify the Constitution, the role of the people vis à vis the Congress remained at issue. During the New York State Constitutional Convention, a resolution was proposed to strip from the Congress the power to lay and collect taxes. Alexander Hamilton sought to allay the delegates' fear that Congress should usurp the power of the people. Hamilton said, addressing the proponent of the resolution, "Here, sir, the people govern. . . ."

Here, sir, the people govern.

Do the people govern or has there been a mutation from a commitment to people to a commitment to self-interest on the part of the governors?

Is the applause meter paramount and the general welfare of the people at best merely tangential?

The government has built an elaborate network of illusions designed to make people believe that their opinions are genuinely wanted and considered—that they participate, in fact, in making the decisions of government. We go to great lengths to sustain the illusion. Prevalent phrases in recent legislation are "citizen participation," "advisory council," "advisory committee," "maximum feasible participation," "public participation," "community participation," and "petition for intervention."

The words are there. But is citizen intervention encouraged or discouraged?

Petitions to intervene in regulatory agency proceedings present a premier example of how best to discourage citizen participation. The rules for intervention in the proceedings of the Atomic Energy Commission are typical. [According to] 2.714 *Intervention* (in adjudicatory proceedings):

> Any person whose interest may be affected by a proceeding and who desires to participate as a party shall file in a written petition . . . for leave to intervene. Any petition shall identify the specific aspect or aspects of the subject matter of the proceedings as to which he wishes to intervene and set forth with particularity both the facts pertaining to his interest and the basis for his contentions with regard to each aspect on which he desires to intervene.

The regulations then continue for seventeen additional sections and subsections. Citizen intervention in the proceedings of other regulatory agencies is equally burdensome.

The people have a right to intervene, though statutory and regulatory language may well include provisions for petitions to intervene. The fact is that proper citizen participation often requires the assistance of an attorney and/or expert witnesses to assist in presenting complicated subject matter. If the citizen needs such assistance and cannot afford an attorney or expert witness, he is effectively denied the right to intervene. The Supreme Court has held that only Congress may authorize the payment of such fees. Congress appears reluctant to do that.

Have Supreme Court decisions furthered opportunities for citizen participation? Recently, the court has acted to limit both the right to sue and class action litigation. The court ruled that citizens and taxpayers have no standing to challenge an alleged pattern of exclusionary zoning because they could not prove that the alleged practice actually harmed them personally. The court ruled that plaintiffs must demonstrate that the injury about which they complained was actual as opposed to arguable.

There is a federal requirement that the amount in controversy must be at least $10,000 before federal court consideration can occur. The Supreme Court has ruled that even if plaintiffs individually satisfied the jurisdictional amount ($10,000), no class action would be allowed unless each member of the class satisfied the jurisdictional amount.

The court has ruled that a person bringing a class action must notify all persons in the class at his own expense. The people want in. How much longer will they tolerate the network of illusions and vacuous rhetoric? What the people want is simple. They want an America as good as its promise.

We want to be in control of our lives—whether we are jungle fighters, craftsmen, company men, or gamesmen—*we* want to be in control, and when government erodes that control, we are discomfited.

I submit that the reinclusion of the people in their government would be a recombinant with predictable and laudable results. It would be the return of a right that was once considered unalienable.

The stakes are too high for government to be a spectator sport.

Council on Foundations Keynote Address

I generally seek inspiration and enlightenment in places other than the great American bumper sticker. But your question to me tonight—or perhaps challenge would be more descriptive—of "should the American notion of civil society be a model that can be exported to the rest of the world, and particularly to the emergent democracies of Eastern Europe and Southern Africa?" does bring to mind one of those little homilies that draws one's eyes and curiosity. "Be patient; God isn't finished with me yet," it declares. Yes, there is much about America's experiment in democracy, as one of the members of the Constitutional Convention called it, that lends itself to emulation, but only if those emulating us are willing to understand that the experiment is not over—and if they are willing to understand that even we who are both participants in and witnesses to the experiment do not always wisely learn from our mistakes.

It is not only appropriate; it is vital that we consider your question in this and other forums, for by honestly, forthrightly considering the notion of exporting our American version of a civil society, we may be able to further our own experiment as well as giving some aid—both financial and otherwise—to other societies.

We cannot escape the cold, cruel reality that democracy has not always been friendly to Black people in America, a reality that should give us some pause before we consider holding ourselves up as a model. But perhaps it is from that rough edge of the experiment that we have the most to share with the emerging democracies in Southern Africa. Some of you may recall the words of Dr. Martin Luther King Jr. in his "Letter from Birmingham Jail":

57

> I am cognizant of the interrelatedness of all communities and states. I cannot sit idly by in Atlanta and not be concerned about what happens in Birmingham. Injustice anywhere is a threat to justice everywhere. We are caught in an inescapable network of mutuality tied in a single garment of destiny. Whatever affects one directly affects all indirectly.

Is that not why each of us is here tonight? "Injustice anywhere is a threat to justice everywhere. . . ."

As we contemplate the question of holding our democracy up as a model, let us be careful to remember that it has taken at least two revolutions to bring us even the imperfect civil society we have today. The first American Revolution freed all white people from the tyranny of a king, but it said nothing about Black people. It was not until Abraham Lincoln and the American Civil War that the second American revolution occurred—this one addressing Black people. Black Americans did not have an easy road to where we are now. As we look to other societies where Black people have not been a part of freedom, we must not forget that work remains to be done here.

I do not intend to dwell entirely on the frailties of our experiment in civil society, for we do have much to offer. Here in this gathering of foundation personnel and grant makers, it is proper to recall one of the insights into our democracy made by the French magistrate Alexis de Tocqueville during his 1831 tour of our country:

> . . . I have often admired the extreme skill with which the inhabitants of the United States succeed in proposing a common object to the exertions of a great many men, and in inducing them voluntarily to pursue it. . . . Amongst democratic nations . . . all the citizens are independent and feeble; they can do hardly anything by themselves, and none of them can oblige his fellowmen to lend him their assistance. They all, therefore, become powerless, if they do not learn voluntarily to help each other.

Please let me underline that last sentence, for it speaks volumes about the notion of the emulation of American civil society. "They all, therefore, become powerless, if they do not learn voluntarily to help each other." And that, of course, is the enduring beauty of foundation work in emerging nations. These voluntary efforts provide strength both here and there, and perhaps set an example for the kind of voluntarism that de Tocqueville had in mind.

Democracy is not easy. If you want nirvana instantly, then democracy is going to be too slow and painful for you. There was much excitement here in 1989 when there seemed to be a catharsis in Eastern Europe. But we now see that democracy has not taken hold in countries not familiar with the agony of the process. When given a choice between food with great control and unlimited freedom with no guarantees, many people will take food. As we watched the recent turmoil in Albania, we saw once again demonstrated a fundamental tenet that democracy requires an economic underpinning—a social and economic infrastructure. You must have private enterprise; you must have private property. When people own their things, work for themselves, they have the great pride necessary for democracy to take hold. If you are impatient, then democracy is not your ideal government mode, because for democracy to take a firm hold requires a laborious effort, a tortuous effort.

Democracy also requires tolerance. Tolerance is, I think, essential to civil order. In a liberal democracy, tolerance is a premier value, because if you are going to be open to people, you particularly have to be able to cut through their differences, accept their differences, and use their differences as a part of the general decision-making act. Differences should not be reasons why we fail. Not at all. Differences should be reasons to succeed. Our cultural diversity and pluralism has its costs but, in the long term, it's worth it.

Civic order requires compromise. It is dangerous to enter the struggle to establish a civil society as a purist—if as a purist you are unwilling to take in others and be flexible. Now, some of you who are students of the American civil rights movement may be thinking that I have painted myself into a tight corner with this talk of patience, compromise, and tolerance. You may recall that in the same essay of Dr. King's that I quoted earlier, he scolds his fellow ministers for their plea to be patient, to be tolerant, to compromise, and to let time take its course. I hope you will understand that Dr. King and I are making the same point. You can have principles that are at the core of your position— we don't kill, we don't maim, and it is essential that we hate bigotry and intolerance. And on these principles I certainly advocate the purist position.

But there are times when you must get off the purist position if you are going to come to a consensus or resolution of the issues. You cannot change the minds of even good men and women overnight—at least not on every issue. If you respect differences, you will also respect the ability of other thoughtful people to struggle internally with a problem and come to an answer that is somewhat different from your own.

It has been thirty-seven years since *Brown v. the Topeka Board of Education*—I doubt that anyone here would be so bold as to tell me that our public school system has achieved perfection after these thirty-seven years. But we have made progress. We have made progress and that progress speaks well to the merits of American civil society. In some ways we have come full circle. Not too many years ago "neighborhood schools" was a battle cry or code word, if you will, of segregationists looking for a polite way to express their beliefs. At this moment in Austin, Texas, our school district wants to redraw its attendance zones. In several areas of the city, you will find coalitions of browns, Blacks, and whites demanding to keep their neighborhood schools *because their neighborhoods are now naturally integrated*! We can pass laws— or change them—overnight. But the lasting changes that come in the hearts and minds of men and women and children are not so quick to come.

It has been my privilege to serve as a trustee of the Kaiser Family Foundation. I have had the opportunity to read an essay about grant making in South Africa written by Dr. Michael Sinclair. One of his observations struck me as particularly worthy of our consideration here tonight. He said that Americans, while quite willing to express their outrage at apartheid, are, on the other hand, not good listeners. This is tragic—though not surprising. Those of us who may have some influence over grants should be constantly careful not to prolong the sadly still alive image of the ugly American. Foundations have much to offer South Africa. The Carnegie Corporation's funding of studies on poor whites in the 1940s and the more recent report on poverty in South Africa are landmark documents. The Ford Foundation has contributed to establishment of a nationwide network of public interest law practices and the Kellogg Foundation is among several who have helped Black South Africans attend previously all-white universities. The Kaiser Foundation is committed to the establishment of a comprehensive primary health-care system in South Africa to serve the majority population and has funded other efforts, including demonstration community-based health projects in different parts of the country.

But let us go into South Africa with our eyes and ears open. Let us go full well knowing that we may find answers to our own problems if we are willing to listen. Certainly, we should not sit idly by in Chicago or Austin and not be concerned about what happens in South Africa. If our version of civil society is worth holding up as a model, we must incorporate into our awareness an aggressive intolerance of injustice anywhere. Our global interconnectedness demands no less.

Civil Rights and Diversity

Many of Barbara Jordan's speeches reflect her views on America's diverse society. These three selected speeches delivered in the latter years of her life offer a challenge to the nation's diverse cultures.

"*E Pluribus Unum:* Myth or Reality? One from Many" is a powerful speech delivered as a commencement address. Jordan was extended countless invitations to speak at every major university in the United States. This speech was given at Northwestern University, September 12, 1993, in Evanston, Illinois.

"How Do We Live with Each Other's Deepest Differences?" is a speech given on race relations in Dayton, Ohio, on June 28, 1990. In this speech she plainly analyzes our nation's documents that promise equal opportunity for all citizens.

Barbara Jordan was awarded the Freedom Award at the National Civil Rights Museum in Memphis, Tennessee, on September 10, 1992. There she delivered the speech titled "Does the Idea of Civil Rights Remain a Good Idea as We Approach the Year 2000 A.D.?"

We are one, we Americans, and we reject any intruder
who seeks to divide us by race or class.
We honor cultural identity.

"Change: From What to What?"
Keynote Address given at the Democratic National Convention
JULY 13, 1992

Northwestern University
Evanston, Illinois
SEPTEMBER 12, 1993

E Pluribus Unum:
Myth or Reality?
One from Many

I am honored by the opportunity to speak to you during this special week. This week is special because you are actualizing a privilege that is not universally shared. At an earlier time in your life, you made the decision that it made more sense to know things rather than to be stupid—that the semiliterate among the inhabitants of a community are not the ones who push the envelope forward but are the ones who inhabit society's basements. Having made that important decision, you sought an institution of higher learning with a no-nonsense reputation—confident that your life would be enhanced by the association.

The credential of a university education moves you instantly into the ranks of the elite. You may protest that such is not the case—that an open society wherein the people rule is a classless society without an upper crust or kings, queens, and rulers. Wrong. Even though we pay lip service to the notion of the power of the people, there is an informal group of decision makers who "call the shots" for policies and programs. If that is true, an obvious question is "Why does not a great democracy as allegedly exists in the United States resist?" The answer is "The right of entry into that governing class is open and available to all who desire to enter." The path to entry is not universally smooth, but *all* are given the right to try. All? All? Is that really true?

Well, the United States of America had the kind of beginning which should eventually validate the prospect of all people having the right to govern. In a historical context, the First Continental Congress met in Philadelphia in 1774. Delegates from twelve colonies. Purpose: To discuss relationships with Britain.

Peyton Randolph of Virginia served as President. Georgia was absent. (Too bad it didn't stay absent long enough.)

May 1775, Second Continental Congress. Purpose: To raise an army and appoint George Washington its Commander in Chief. Also it adopted the "Declaration of the Crises and necessity of taking up Arms."

June 1776, Congress appointed Thomas Jefferson to head a committee to draft a Declaration of Independence, which was adopted on July 4, 1776, by the Congress meeting in New York.

All were not represented initially. My ancestors were not involved in any of these deliberations. Reason? We had not achieved the status of personhood—we were considered chattel, property—without mind, heart, or soul. The Declaration was stunning: "We hold these truths to be self-evident, that all men are created equal . . . endowed by their creator with certain unalienable rights," among which are "life, liberty, and the pursuit of happiness." To secure these rights, governments are instituted, deriving their just powers from the consent of the governed. That consent gave the government its legitimacy but— what about me?

That great Democrat, Thomas Jefferson, was uneasy about Black-white equality. On one occasion—even after Lincoln's Emancipation Proclamation, Jefferson voiced his discomfort in saying, "I feel like I've got the wolf by the ears. We can neither hold him nor safely let him go."

Our beginnings were uncomfortable and to a certain extent we Black Americans are still trying to find a comfort zone. But in the face of our oppressed beginnings—we never lost faith that America could be made to work for us.

How was this inelegant beginning transformed into a government which celebrated diversity? This transformation was aided and abetted by a public philosophy which is honored by each American. If such a philosophy is absent, conflict is predictable. That public philosophy includes an unambiguous tolerance of differences in others. There is no peace without that virtue.

In the American experience, we have witnessed bloodshed. The Civil War was our bloodiest. We have experienced ethnic and cultural strife. To paraphrase William Faulkner's remarks upon accepting the Nobel Prize for literature, we have done more than endure this bloodshed and strife; we have in many senses prevailed. Our history is not yet complete. We certainly cannot declare victory, but we can draw profound encouragement from history.

The United Nations recently released a human development report, whose chief author said that "the United States has a commendable record on human rights and affirmative action. It is an open society, with nondiscrimination written into law, and there is a media that keeps pressure on the issue. And there have been tremendous improvements in integration since the 1960s."

As we consider the stubborn, lingering indicia of racism, it may be useful to ponder the questions of how ethnic groups have contributed to the whole community—whether they can help to sustain the soul of the nation. It is useful to engage in a certain amount of speculation. Are the feelings that we hold from our parochial perspectives at all similar to the feelings of those who knew from a distance that the institution of slavery existed in their time in America? Are our feelings at all similar to those held by the men and women who knew from afar of the systematic executions of Jews in Europe in the 1930s and 1940s? End of speculation.

Slavery is now unconstitutional in the United States, and Nazi Germany has been destroyed as it at one time existed. But like the Phoenix, neo-Nazis and skinheads make our lives uncomfortable. If we are in a similar position to those who knew of the existence of slavery and those who knew of the European Holocaust, are there lessons to be learned? Can we avoid mistakes that were made by our predecessors? Can we get to the fulcrum of the matter and end the strife of the 1990s in short order? Can we cobble *unum* to *e pluribus*?

I do not advocate that we paper over the conflicts which plague us. At the same time, I do not advocate that we sit idly by as men and women and children are harmed physically and mentally for no other reason than where they happened to be born or where they happen to live. We need to bring into our deliberations the historical perspective of knowing that there have been parallels to conflicts presently witnessed. Certainly not exact, but it is imperative that we exercise our marvelous human gifts of deliberation and reasoning to learn something from the past.

Does the American experience of segregation and integration have any lessons to teach us?

My proposition is that we have learned from our past. Our experience with race, slavery, civil rights, and the rule of the law is unlike that of any other nation on earth. One distinction is that, notwithstanding our differences, there is a homogeneity. We speak of race more than we speak of ethnicity. We don't have deep cultural differences that exist in other parts of the world. In a sense, we are all immigrants. We are able to point to a common code of decency and civility that enables us to be a nation, that enables us to embrace the many things that we hold in common, while allowing us to acknowledge that we do have differences. Yet those differences do not and must not irreparably divide. Instead, they should and most often do allow us to foster a rich and vibrant society.

American history is certainly not an unblemished record of peaceful problem solving. I mentioned earlier the United Nations' human development report. After saying very positive things about the United States, the authors issued this warning: "But the United States still has grave problems, which only shows how far other countries have to go." Franklin Balch, professor of political science at Southern Methodist University, reminds me that we have our own history of ethnic cleansing carried out against the American Indians. Some of this was inadvertent, through the transmission of white people's diseases during otherwise civil meetings to exchange or barter food and merchandise. But some of it was intentional genocide, through deliberate transmission of diseases, such as when pox was put in blankets given or sold to the Indians. One of the saddest chapters of our history was the Trail of Tears, the forced migration at the turn of the nineteenth century of the Cherokee Indians from their chosen homeland onto reservations picked for them by white men.

The evidence is mounting about another form of deliberate disregard for the lives and health of minorities. I refer to what is called environmental racism: landfills, sewage plants, toxic waste incinerators, and other sources of toxic pollution that tend to be located in low-income and minority areas. This environmental racism creates another loop of the cycle of poverty. Struggling families who have managed to get a foot in the door by owning a small home find their property values lowered because of their proximity to waste sites. They can't afford to move unless they can sell their homes, which are virtually worthless because of the potential for contamination. And if they are unfortunate enough to have their situation complicated by having one or more family members afflicted with an environmental illness—conditions that occur at higher than normal rates close to these waste sites—they are beaten down even further.

I do not summarily judge that each and every owner or stockholder in an industrial waste–generating facility located in a minority neighborhood is guilty of intentional genocide. The roots of environmental racism often go deep into the histories of zoning codes and the inability of those codes to keep up with growing populations. But we are a sophisticated enough society to address complex problems. Environmental racism is new.

American history has many chapters of racial tension and outright racial violence. We can see a pattern of ethnic groups establishing their identity, then turning against new ethnic groups that follow them to their region. Of course, some of the most bitter clashes have been on religious grounds rather than ethnic grounds, with anti-Semitism being the most widely known. We also saw strong anti-Irish and anti-Catholic feelings peak during and shortly after a large wave of Irish immigrants in the late nineteenth century.

What is it, then, that gives any country the strength to endure as a nation? Is it as Maya Angelou once remarked about America that "We really are fifteen countries, and it's really remarkable that each of us thinks we represent the *real* America. The Midwesterner in Kansas, the Black American in Durham— both are certain they are the real American"? Or is it as former President Carter once said, "We become not a melting pot, but a beautiful mosaic. Different people, different beliefs, different yearnings, different hopes, different dreams"? Or is it as the late Justice Thurgood Marshall once said, "If America is a melting pot, the Negro either did not get into the pot or didn't melt down"?

We are not a perfect society. We are still practicing, still learning how to make this creation called democracy work. In the Human Development Index, I note that while white Americans rank first in the world, American Blacks rank thirty-first and American Hispanics rank thirty-fifth. We can easily point to the symptoms of the failures of our experiment—one need look no further than the Los Angeles riots of last year. But more often, a hard look at the very heart of American society will not find the explosive situation that was Los Angeles. More often, we find a complex set of circumstances with a set of complex people working on those circumstances—people who realize that our country's fate will comport with its original intent only if the worth, the value of each of its citizens, is respected.

Daniel Bell in 1947 wrote that "A dispassionate view of the American scene shows that the greatest store of hate against Negroes, the most oppressed group, lies among the poor whites." Class, not race, being the dominant factor.

In *Faces at the Bottom of the Well*, that book's author, Derrick Bell, contends that "racism is an integral, permanent, and indestructible component of this society." Blacks are doomed to fail, he argues, as long as a majority of whites don't understand that the fates of the two races are inextricably linked. Among middle-class citizens of both races, there is an understanding of this commonality of fate. And among those who are poor, of both races, there is hatred. I do not agree with Derrick Bell's dire assessment.

I am optimistic about the future of the United States. I refuse to view racism as a permanent component of our society. I see progress. I see progress in the policies of President Clinton and, for instance, Texas Governor Ann Richards. We may quarrel over details, but these are two prominent politicians who have based their policies on inclusion, rather than exclusion. It is no accident that their cabinets include women and men and Blacks and browns, because they have worked for inclusion throughout their careers.

To be intellectually honest, however, we must ask questions that challenge this optimistic view. In *The Truly Disadvantaged*, William Julius Wilson argues that for all of our radical changes in public policy in the last forty years, we have not only failed to solve the problems of the urban ghetto; we have made them worse.

Were the Los Angeles riots only a precursor of what is to come? Has a class structure been created in America in which race is no longer the key difference? When we look at small town America, we see that the middle class has overcome many of the fears and prejudices of the past while the lower class has maintained racial hatred. Are we looking at a symptom of a nationwide problem that we need to face before it explodes in a manner similar to Eastern Europe?

Should we look at other parts of the world to see if there are lessons that can be used to avoid a class struggle that will once again cause blood to be shed on American soil—or perhaps American streets and sidewalks?

This is certainly not a new idea. In the seventeenth century, for instance, John Locke warned of the impossibility of government being all-inclusive. He argued that we should be ever mindful of this, or face the end of the government that ignored its fallibility, to be replaced by another attempt.

As a government we set an ambitious agenda for ourselves. We placed our faith in people with their limitless human potential and human possibility. We set standards which could be more easily pronounced than achieved.

Are all men and women created equal as the American Declaration of Independence asserts? The honest answer is no. And we continue to have a problem with equality because equality is perceived as a threat. We generally want to be safe and secure, and the requirement of equality is too often seen as a threat to that security.

But as a nation, we continue to try to live up to our historical promises, and foremost among them is the promise of equality of opportunity. It was decided very early in its history that all Americans are entitled to equality of opportunity. It has not been an easy promise to fulfill. Slavery is, of course, a huge and ugly stain on our history. But we have continued to struggle for equality of opportunity. The Thirteenth Amendment to the Constitution, abolishing slavery, was added in 1865, yet it took more than 100 years for Congress to pass a Civil Rights Act. One part of that act is a promise that Congress made more than 100 years earlier to former slaves that they would be treated fairly in the workplace and in other contractual relationships.

As an American who is Black and female, I cannot sit here today and hold up this 100-year delay in equality of opportunity as an example of the way things should work. The American experience is a valid lesson. It has been a tiring, yet glorious struggle. And you in this community of scholars have an obligation for leadership in this struggle—you who will become a part of the governing elite.

We Americans were so fascinated by the phrase *e pluribus unum* that we struck it on a coin and made it the great seal and symbol of our definition. Is that notion dead? A victim of an internecine struggle? Or does it remain alive and promising? Ralph Ellison, the author of the classic *The Invisible Man*, wrote that "America is woven of many strands; I would recognize them and let it so remain. . . . Our fate is to become one, and yet many."

Our strength is rooted in our diversity. History bears witness to that statement. But that diversity is rife with strain, tension, and doubt. A perfect union has not been formed. One can go to the megacity of Los Angeles or the tiny rural town in the flatlands of Arkansas to see our imperfections. Some Americans of all races still feel the wretchedness that Frederick Douglass, a former slave, described. America's mission was and still is to take its diversity and mold it into a cohesive and coherent whole that would espouse virtues and values essential to the maintenance of civil order. There is nothing easy about that mission. But it is not mission impossible.

Solutions we develop will not always be the correct ones. As Reinhold Niebuhr warned, we should question whether democracy is the correct solution for every nation. Just as there is room for diversity in America, there should be room for diversity in the world. As Ellison suggested, it is our fate to be both one and many. That is the formula for both peace, civility, and comforting worldwide stability. *E pluribus unum*—must not die. Heroic efforts are essential to keep it alive.

How Do We Live with Each Other's Deepest Differences?

That question is raised in a document called the Williamsburg Charter, which was signed by many people (including myself). The purpose of the document was to state a reaffirmation of our faith in and commitment to the First Amendment of the United States Constitution. It is noted that the question "How do we live with each other's deepest differences?" is one of the world's most pressing questions in the late twentieth century. We are indeed a polyglot nation. Our hues are many; our origins multiple; our language reflective of place; our hair sometimes challenging identity. In the midst of this diversity, one is quickly aware that most of these differences mentioned are of a surface nature, cosmetic. Are such differences likely to lead to conflict and unstable communities? Let's withhold an answer to the questions for the moment. Our pluralism contains these differences, but notwithstanding, there remains within and among us a common strain which binds and strengthens.

A common strain does not require that I deny or reject my culture or my heritage. The community within pluralism requires that my difference be seen and acknowledged, and if not accommodated, at a minimum, tolerated. This point is made in the charter mentioned. "Pluralism must not be confused with, and is in fact endangered by, philosophical and ethical indifference. Commitment to strong, clear philosophical and ethical ideas need not imply either intolerance or opposition to democratic pluralism. On the contrary, democratic pluralism requires an agreement to be locked in public argument over disagreements of consequence within the bonds of civility." In other words, if we have differences so deep and profound that they threaten public order and civility, they should be brought out into the open—discussed and debated, and if possible resolved. If resolution is not possible, every effort should be made to reach a consensus through compromise.

Why is it that today—125 years after the Civil War, thirty-six years after the decision in *Brown versus the Board of Education of Topeka, Kansas*, twenty-six years after the Civil Rights Act of 1964, twenty-five years after the Voting Rights Act of 1965—why is it that after all of these years of addressing the problem of race in American life, we are assembled in Dayton, Ohio, talking about Black/white relations and building bridges in a divided city? What is the problem? Why do we see an apparent resurgence of racism across the face of America—especially on college campuses? What's wrong? White America, what's bugging you? Is America an experiment which failed?

This country made some grandiose promises. We promised liberty, freedom, and equality to everybody. No one was to be excluded from the blessings of liberty. As a nation we have done well actualizing the promise of liberty (the absence of restraint) and freedom (the absence of coercion). America is the land of the free and is the model for nascent democracies around the world.

What about equality? Has that promise been fulfilled? Do the words of the Declaration of Independence, "All men are created equal," ring true? No. The real answer is no. We have a problem in this country with the ideas of equality. The problem begins when we try to define the word. What does equality mean? Must all of us have exactly the same amount of the same thing? Is someone going to take some of what I have so that the distribution of money and goods is equal? The point is that equality is viewed as a threat. People generally want to be secure in what they have, and a requirement of equality threatens that security.

We continue as a nation to try to make good our historical promises, particularly the promise of equality of *opportunity*. It was decided very early in the history of this country that all American citizens are entitled to equality of opportunity. That fact has made achievement and fulfillment of that promise difficult. Slavery is an ugly stain on our history. Frederick Douglass was a slave who, after teaching himself to write, wrote a narrative about slavery. Few can read it without experiencing a lump in the throat or a tear in the eye. In case you have never read or heard this work, I will read to you the first three paragraphs.

. . .

Human subjugation was an intolerable condition.

The Thirteenth Amendment was added to the Constitution of the United States in 1865, abolishing slavery. But that was not enough to fulfill the promise of equality. In 1866, Congress passed a Civil Rights Act. Section 1981 of that act is a promise that Congress made more than a century ago to newly freed slaves—that they would be treated fairly in the workplace and in other contractual relationships. There was established a public policy against racial bias, enforced and undiluted.

A Supreme Court decision handed down last summer raised questions about the stability of this policy. It is known as the *Patterson* case. Brenda Patterson sued her employer under the 1866 act, charging racial harassment on the job. The court held that the 1866 Civil Rights Act prohibits race discrimination in *hiring* workers, but is not applicable to harassment on the job nor to firing or promotion denials because of race prejudices.

I believe this is an artificial distinction. The *Patterson* decision has caused the dismissal of at least ninety-six claims of race discrimination in the past eight months.

Our promise is equal opportunity. Fact? Or illusion? In another Supreme Court case, the *Wards Cove* decision handed down last year, the court shifted the burden of proof from employers to employees in cases involving practices that operate to exclude minorities and women. The court held that the employer had the burden of production of evidence that the practice was a business necessity, but the employee always had the burden of persuasion. This distinction makes it difficult and expensive for victims of discrimination to challenge the barriers they face.

Equal opportunity. Illusion? Or fact? There is yet a third decision: *Martin versus Wilks*. The Supreme Court held that consent decrees settling job discrimination cases may be reopened in future lawsuits. In the wake of that decision, long-standing decrees have been challenged in new lawsuits. The inherent possibility is endless litigation.

What can or should be done if these Supreme Court actions impede further gains in civil rights and affirmative action programs? Shortly after this 1989 series of Supreme Court decisions, President Bush said, "If the decisions actually turn out to hamper Civil Rights enforcement . . . obviously I would want to take steps to remedy the situation."

There is now evidence that these decisions have had an adverse impact on Americans who are seeking legal redress against unfair treatment at work. Several members of Congress have responded by introducing the Civil Rights Act of 1990, new legislation designed to restore and strengthen civil rights protections. The United States Senate began debate on this measure this week. This bill should pass.

I enlist a winning coalition to drive the American Dream to an inexorable and glorious conclusion. The pillars I enlist are the government, business, and the church. George Mason wrote in 1776, "No free government, or the blessings of liberty, can be preserved to any people, but by a firm adherence to justice, moderation, temperance, frugality, and virtue, and by frequent recurrence to fundamental principles."

In my opinion, the coalition of government and business, with their ubiquitous presence, and the church, as guardian of our virtue, could form a partnership made in heaven.

Freedom Award
National Civil Rights Museum
Memphis, Tennessee
SEPTEMBER 10, 1992

Does the Idea of Civil Rights Remain a Good Idea as We Approach the Year 2000 A.D.?

There is a myriad of words and phrases which bump up against and crowd the concept of civil rights. Words like "fight for, struggle, wrest, inherent, individual, autonomy, responsible, citizen, government, laws, freedom, King, Kennedy, and Johnson." Over the years these words have enjoyed uneven salience. We have seen paroxysms of attention and inattention to the movement of the idea of civil rights. A history of America could be written by documenting that movement. And yet these decades of halting progress followed by stalemate followed by progress have left many of us feeling incomplete and unfulfilled. Why has this issue been so difficult to resolve? Why have successive civil rights bills not done the job they were allegedly designed to do?

One thing is obvious. America has a difficult time reconciling its egalitarian rhetoric with its self-absorbed reality. We have an awkward time just defining words like *rights*, *equality*. Try it. What are rights? What is a right? My students (all of whom are graduate students) stumble with those definitions. They usually end their effort with something like "Well . . . you know."

I define *rights* or a *right* as "that which is *due* to anyone by tradition, law, or nature." That is not a perfect definition but it covers most of the necessary questions. The word *due* implies an entitlement. There are some things to which one is entitled without question. Here, I am *not* talking about any government benefits. I speak here of fundamental rights—life, liberty, and the pursuit of

75

happiness. These are human rights to which there is universal entitlement, without exception. It was William Lloyd Garrison who in speaking of rights said, "Wherever there is a human being, I see God-given rights inherent in that being whatever may be the sex or complexion."

The content of human rights is unarguable. The quarrels begin when one places the word *civil* before the word *rights*. *Civil* invokes relationships between individuals. It encompasses how we deal with each other and the state, the government. *Civil* includes both social and legal relations.

This country was founded on the new and extraordinary notion that all people are equal. That idea can be found in two of America's founding documents: the Declaration of Independence, 1776, and the Constitution of the United States, 1868. (That second date, as you perhaps know, is *not* the date of ratification of the Constitution—1787—but the year of ratification of the Fourteenth Amendment to the Constitution.) Equality was made a part of the Constitution only after we fought a war with ourselves. We still did not grasp the full meaning of *civil rights*.

It was tried (with the approval of the Supreme Court) to separate former slaves from others. The case of *Plessy versus Ferguson* documents that statement. The good news is that [*Plessy*] was not a unanimous decision of the Court. Justice John Marshall Harlan, in his dissent, sounded with clarity the rationale which would render inoperable and immoral the doctrine of separate but equal. He said, "In view of the Constitution, in the eye of the law, there is in this country no superior, dominant, ruling class of citizens. There is no caste here. Our Constitution is colorblind, and neither knows nor tolerates classes among citizens. In respect of civil rights, all citizens are equal before the law. The humblest is the peer of the most powerful." The year of that decision was 1896. Four years later the twentieth century began.

The year was 1900. The occasion—the Pan-African conference. Location—London. Audience—the nations of the world. Speaker—William Edward Burghardt Du Bois, colloquially known as W.E.B. Du Bois—1886–1963. The message—"The problem of the twentieth century is the problem of the color line."

Du Bois lived long enough to change that chilling message, had he so desired. But he didn't. The message stands unaltered by history and remains both a challenge and an indictment. Try as it has over the past 200 plus years, America has not successfully come to grips with us. It is correct to note that Du Bois was prescient in identifying the stark and singular problem which would dog the twentieth century: color. The majority community has adopted, over the years, a number of strategies for dealing with the problem. The latest seems to be—pretend it's not there. Ignore it—or adopt strategies to suppress it. We are witnessing a presidential contest in which the rhetoric appears to distance the candidate from a group of American citizens, disproportionately, negatively impacted by this long national economic malaise. To ignore does not solve—it only postpones. We must deal effectively with those outcomes which are a direct result of the problem of the color line. One strategy which has stood well the test of time is—educate the uneducated.

The founders of this country were thoughtful, well-read men (history records no role for the women of the period). James Madison, Benjamin Franklin, Thomas Jefferson, John Locke, Newton, Bacon, Rousseau, and others. What emerged from their deliberation was a new nation in which the citizens were given the responsibility for governing themselves. What a daunting task. An experiment, a democracy. A democratic republic. Self-government. People power. What about color? The problem? Response? Just declare that those of African descent in the new nation are not people—are not recognized as "whole persons."

These men of the enlightenment—these well-read, learned men—wallowed in darkness when it came to the problem. It is a somewhat dark curiosity that at this moment, when democracy seems to be the governmental form of choice, the average American appears grossly disinterested. Democracy needs the nourishment and nurturing of its citizens. Inattention kills it.

An enlightened citizenry is an indispensable ingredient of the infrastructure of democracy. Each citizen must become informed. If the individual does not assume that responsibility, he or she may forfeit his or her rights. Some may argue that the requirement of *universal* education has a dilutive effect on the quality of the education offered. The majority of us reject that notion and reaffirm that the opportunity to learn must be available to all. *All mean all—* the only limiting factor is ability. That education is a vital underpinning of democracy has long been known. If the civil rights initiative is to regain momentum, those who lead must passionately embrace the knowledge base of the future.

Writing in 1846, the renowned educator Horace Mann told us that

> They, then, who knowingly withhold sustenance from a newborn child, and he dies, are guilty of infanticide. And, by the same reasoning, they who refuse to enlighten the intellect of a rising generation, are guilty of degrading the human race!
>
> They who refuse to train up children in the way they should go, are training up incendiaries and madmen to destroy property and life, and to invade and pollute the sanctuaries of society.

Our task is to enlighten the intellect of a rising generation. Those efforts have practical, material benefits. We have all seen statistics and reports about the earning power of a diploma or a degree. The United States Census Bureau reports some startling figures about differences in earning power based solely on education.

Is there a difference other than a material reward between the educated life and the uneducated? Yes. One who is educated has certain civilizing tendencies and is open to the inner reality of others. He or she has a tolerance for diversity and supports an open marketplace for ideas and debate. Those who are educated recognize that the pursuit of truth never ends.

Our diversity and pluralism is not without costs. Some suggest it pulls down the learning curve. Our response is "Tough." All have a right to learn. It is a civil right.

Frederick Douglass was born a slave. You know the highlights of his story. He taught himself to read, educated himself for the most part, escaped from slavery, and became a great American. He was an advisor to President Lincoln and consul general to Haiti. He also was a tireless worker for equal rights for Blacks and for women. One of the most insightful passages of his autobiography, *The Life and Times of Frederick Douglass*, comes not from Douglass himself, but from a message that he says came from the white man who was his so-called master:

> Learning will spoil the best nigger in the world. If he learns to read the Bible, it will forever unfit him to be a slave. He should know nothing but the will of his master, and learn to obey it. As to himself, learning will do him no good, but a great deal of harm, making him disconsolate and unhappy. If you teach him how to read, he'll want to know how to write, and this accomplished, he'll be running away with himself.

Douglass's reaction was a very simple one. "Very well," he recollected as he thought. "Knowledge unfits a child to be a slave . . . and from that moment I understood the direct pathway from slavery to freedom."

Does the idea of civil rights remain a good idea as we approach the year 2000 A.D.? Or are we a generation of naysayers who would mock the sacrifices of those who pioneered?

Has the American dream of *e pluribus unum* died? Was the promise of a colorblind society a fraud? Are the words "multiculturalism" and "political correctness" code words for a new reality of a nation in which separateness and ethnic chauvinism are to be celebrated? I say no. No. A thousand times NO.

I am not ready to give up on our experiment in democracy. It was and continues to be a bold experiment. I believe the motto "from many, one." Our nineteenth-century visitor from France, de Tocqueville, with awe and puzzlement described America this way:

> a society formed of all nations of the world . . . people having different languages, beliefs, opinions: in a word, a society without roots, without memories, without prejudices, without routines, without common ideas, without a national character, yet a hundred times happier than our own.

What could make this miscellany into a single society?

Each and every one of us can make this society whole. An African-American professor at Harvard commented in this month's edition of *Forbes* magazine that this is simultaneously the best of times and the worst of times for Black Americans. I agree. But I also know the outcome. Our heritage dictates that we make America work for us . . . and we will.

Ethics

As holder of the Lyndon Baines Johnson Centennial Chair in National Policy, Barbara Jordan taught the course titled Political Value and Ethics. She was later appointed by Texas Governor Ann Richards as Special Counsel for Ethics. Barbara Jordan will be remembered for her many "firsts" and other achievements; she will best be remembered for her high ethical standards.

The following speeches, "The Rebirth of Ethics—A Pervasive Challenge" and "Ethical Dilemmas of Leadership," reflect Jordan's ethical values and beliefs.

There are ethical dilemmas in leadership. You may be armed with all the facts and all of the latest management theories, but unless you consider the moral dimension, I contend that your decisions and your leadership will be hollow right down to the core.

"Ethical Dilemmas of Leadership"
MARCH 1, 1994

Association for Investment Management and Research
San Antonio, Texas
MAY 5, 1992

The Rebirth of Ethics—
A Pervasive Challenge

I am most pleased and delighted that you have asked me to talk to you. I am pleased because it is always good to be asked to speak to those I do not daily encounter. It warms the heart to know that men and women whose daily focus is upon the wise handling of money have an interest in more than the bottom line as it is expressed in dollars and cents.

Given the subject you have asked me to discuss, I know instantly that you realize that ethics is everybody's business. You have requested that I talk about "The Rebirth of Ethics—A Pervasive Challenge."

I approach with no small trepidation anytime I hear or see the word "rebirth." Quite simply, rebirth implies that something wasn't right the first time around, that we have junked it and started over. When the subject is ethics, our history is pockmarked with periods of attention and inattention. I don't have to remind you that we are only a few years removed from another so-called rebirth of ethics. In the mid- and late-1970s, with the scurrilous behavior of Watergate fresh on our minds, ethics became a popular topic upon which to be well-versed.

All across the country, public agencies and private businesses began requiring key personnel to attend ethics courses. Others made very public displays of inviting prominent ministers, professors, and other experts on ethical behavior—ethicists—to address seminars or lead weekend management retreats. Now we would seem to be entering another cycle of the same attempts at behavioral adjustment.

I do not mention this to suggest that we do not now need to talk about a rebirth of ethics. Far from it. I applaud you for studying the problem and investing your time in this manner. You are investment managers. People trust you with the future of their most sacred property—their money. I think your dividends will be great. Let us hope that you discover a sustained yield and not just a one-time bonus! (To employ some of the language of your trade.)

As I have met with and talked to various groups with many different interests, the pervasive complaint that I have heard about government is that it doesn't work. Nothing is moving. Nothing is happening. We have reached gridlock. The feeling is strong that the people in positions of trust are not responding to the trust placed in them by the American electorate. People have, in a very profound way, lost faith, trust, and confidence in the people chosen to be our primary policymakers.

I know that the word *crisis* is much overused. But I do not think it inappropriate to apply it to the deterioration of trust that we are witnessing today. Democracy has a central requirement of an infrastructure if it is to work. A key ingredient of that infrastructure is trust—and that is what is missing in 1992.

We must demand behavior from those who serve us that is worthy of our trust and confidence, and we must not be shy about stating our demands for such ethical conduct.

The man or woman in a public policy leadership role of course has a responsibility to serve the public. The requirements of service are multiple, but if one is to be excellent, then he or she must act on behalf of the larger, common good and reject any private interest. That is so basic I am almost embarrassed to say it. Those in office today should realize that they are trustees who have failed to exercise a proper amount of care. If you know anything about the law of trusts, you know that a trustee is held to the highest standard of care recognized in law. So it is with the holder of the public trust.

I find it somewhat fascinating how we pick symbols to express our frustration and loss of confidence. Symbols are just what the word means: symbolic, lacking in substance. The symbol, however, is often reflective of [a] troubling matter which has profound substance. Check overdrafts of members of Congress from the now-closed House Bank are symbolic of personal financial mismanagement and disregard for the rules of law and order which govern the average American citizen; chauffeur-driven cars—symbolic of an elitism which is antithetical to a democracy; use of a government airplane for a trip to the doctor or ski lodge—symbolic of a disregard to protect the U.S. taxpayer from unnecessary outlays or expenses; term limitation petitions—symbolic of those who have become calcified in office and are no longer responsive to the public weal. Too many perks and privileges befitting a king or queen or potentate but not a public servant in an American democracy.

The House banking imbroglio, the use of government planes for private purposes by former White House Chief of Staff John Sununu, among others; the extensive use of limousines by high government officials; and—here in

Texas—the use of government phones for private purposes. If our government were doing what we expect—if it were addressing the problems of the homeless, if it were engaging in meaningful debate on what to do about our decaying cities, if it were seeking solutions to the debate over abortion rather than calling names, if it were taking courageous steps to fight AIDS and to improve the health of our youngsters born into families below the poverty line—then I suspect we would not waste our time on the symbols of misuse of power. When the public trust is misused, it must be addressed. But if our government were functioning the way it should be, abuse of trust would not be so widespread. I am convinced that you and I, the American people, are capable of forgiving mistakes if they are made in the ethical pursuit of excellence.

Our country cannot sufficiently, successfully govern if we cannot trust others—and in particular those we elect and endow with the public trust. Ethics requires that those we elect hold that grant of authority as a personal trust. And we as beneficiaries need to be able to look at the people we elect and say, "I'm just delighted that you are where you are and that I've placed trust in you."

Yes, there is a rebirth of ethics. The environment of ethics has shifted. It requires an extraordinary ability to change and to search one's heart and soul for the answers to each new situation and question.

When I speak to graduating college seniors, I sometimes quote that delightful and insightful essay, "All I Ever Needed to Know I Learned in Kindergarten." We seem to have an abundance of elected leaders today who did not learn their kindergarten lessons very well. And thus, when confronted with a new situation that demands some thought, some consideration of the trust placed in them, they do not have a rather simple set of standards on which to fall back. Instead, they fall back on sophistry. They delight in seemingly plausible explanations for implausible behavior. And yet, to use another reference to kindergarten, we seem to be able, as did the children in the fairy tale, to sooner or later figure out that the emperors are without clothing.

It is very easy to spot which emperors are naked if we keep in mind that the people are the masters and the government is the servant.

The public leader cannot be elitist. As you may know, I have the honor of serving as Governor Ann Richards's special adviser on ethics in state government. In this role I have sought to communicate this public service philosophy I have talked about this morning. There is nothing complicated or difficult about ethics. It's about values. It's about right and wrong behavior. It's about the common good—the good we all hold in common, notwithstanding race or gender.

I would guess that some of you are forming a question as I speak. That is, do I hold public servants to a higher standard than persons in, say, financial management? The answer, truthfully, is yes, *unless, of course, it is my finances* that you are managing! I do not mean that as a flip comment. Actually, I think it illustrates one of the principles of a democracy that I have been discussing. When we elect someone, we are bestowing upon him or her a trusteeship that should be motivated by the public interest.

When I employ a financial manager, or a doctor, certainly I demand high standards from that person. But I employ them from the marketplace in order that they may represent my interest. If they do not meet my standards, if they do not in my judgment represent my interests in the best possible manner— that is, to my greatest benefit—then I am free to return to the marketplace and seek another practitioner. It doesn't work quite that way with public office, but almost. If I am not happy with the man or woman in whom I have entrusted public office, I must work cooperatively and democratically to convince my neighbors and my fellow citizens to join me at the polls to throw the rascal out. It may be that some of my neighbors feel that they have been served quite well. That is the difference between the free marketplace and the free ballot.

That is where your association comes into play. It is good—no, it is more than good—it is admirable and highly commendable that you as an association seek to instill the highest of ethical standards in your profession. Yours and other professional associations like yours protect the amateurs like me, so that if I am unhappy with the way you handle my finances, at least I will have some finances left to take to the next associate I seek.

Your profession has its problems too. And there are parallels between public and private life. Some people are apparently unable to resist the temptations that come with access to power or money. You may think it amusing for me to quote from John Dean, the special assistant to Richard Nixon during Watergate. I would simply point out that he very aptly titled his book *Blind Ambition* and that the first chapter of the book was called "Reaching for the Top, Touching the Bottom." All too often, even those who are elected professing the highest ideals develop an arrogance of power. They exhibit behavior that is not worthy of those holding public trust.

We cannot expect excellence in leadership, whether it be in public office or in a private profession, unless we demand it. We, as citizens—you as professionals—must clearly articulate what excellence means to us, then we must hold our leaders to those articulated ideals. And we must be relentless. We should not relax simply because the public official has run on a platform that speaks of excellence. We must demand that he or she live up to it. You should not relax just because your association has published its fine statement of purpose.

We are not asking the impossible. Our leaders must be men and women of substance. They should believe in something and have values—moral qualities like optimism, courage, and fairness—at their core.

Yes, we should expect that our leaders will make mistakes—after all, we do not live perfect lives. But we must let them know that we will judge them by how they recover from their mistakes. That is not too much to ask. The truth of the matter is that "All we ever really needed to know, we did, in fact, learn in kindergarten." Think about that.

Lectureship in Student Leadership
Texas Union
Austin, Texas
MARCH 1, 1994

Ethical Dilemmas
of Leadership

I am extremely delighted to have this opportunity to present this talk as the designated hitter for this year's Lectureship in Student Leadership. I have a good reason to be "extremely delighted." You will be in charge soon, and I can retire. I understand that the purpose of this lectureship is to give you a chance to explore the multiple dimensions of leadership (i.e., its philosophies, styles, challenges, responsibilities, content, and essence). You ask for my participation in taking a look at the historical and political perspectives which attend the "ethical dilemmas" of leadership.

It is my firm view that the qualities of leadership you display as a student will not be appreciably different from those you show as an adult. The only differences are those which result from the process of maturation.

It is a given that you are not yet fully formed (I have no doubt that some of you will disagree with that statement): certain exemptions and allowances are made for your non-age. But nothing exempts you from responsibility for your actions—personal responsibility. Your age of innocence is fleeting and the future depends on what you write on the blank slate you are given at birth. (I understand genetic markings help to determine what follows, but to deal with that is beyond the scope of this talk.) You are the final author of the content of your life. What kind of person do you want to be? Do you want to be the leader of the pack, or will you be content to be a contributor of substance to the outcome?

I graduated from high school before most of you here were even an idea. I then enrolled in Texas Southern University. I was sixteen. There was a student body election about to get under way. I located the campaign office, picked up the necessary forms, and filed for president. I had made the decision to lead. Of course, I was later informed by the dean of women that a freshman could not be President. But I had made a choice: to lead.

Leadership has its requirements. One prime requirement is self-confidence. If you do not believe that you have the capacity, the capability to do the job required, you have veered into the wrong situation. That self-confidence must stop far short of arrogance and a belief that you have all of the answers. No one has all of the answers. Those who lead are sometimes faced with situations which require a choice between two equally balanced alternatives or equally undesirable ones. That's the conventional definition of a dilemma. There is nothing new about decision makers [or] leaders confronting dilemmas.

Leaders have faced difficult choices for at least as long as scribes have been present to record their actions. Some of those choices have moral and ethical content. Ethics and leadership go back even farther than recorded history and trace their origins to roughly the same moment in the development of human beings. Our earliest literature—that which synopsizes the fables and history handed down by word of mouth for countless generations—reminds us that ethical dilemmas are not a modern phenomenon. One of the first leaders to be chronicled in the Bible, Abraham, was given perhaps the most excruciating ethical dilemma found in religious history—to prove his loyalty to God by sacrificing his son, Isaac.

Another Abraham, Lincoln, knew that freeing the slaves would divide the nation. Yet he knew that if slaves were not freed, hatred and prejudice and that awful, official sanction of one citizen's subjugation of another would continue and perhaps divide the nation even more agonizingly.

Leadership does not lend itself to easy ethical solutions. An effective leader will agonize over the impact and effect of a decision, notwithstanding the size of his [or] her constituency. History does not promise that the choices you make in your leadership role will be entirely right or entirely wrong. Gandhi, whose contributions to human rights and the dignity of all races are unexcelled, chose to turn to a life of celibacy without consulting his wife. His biographers tell us that his work for the good of all cost his children the presence of a father.

Former Senator J. William Fulbright faced an unusual ethical dilemma. As the junior senator from Arkansas, he knew that he could not be reelected from a still-segregated Southern state if he followed his conscience and supported civil rights legislation. Thus, the name of this man who championed international human rights can be found on some of the most racist, demeaning documents and domestic legislation of the 1960s. Was he right or was he wrong?

We can find examples of ethical dilemmas where the solutions chosen were less clouded with ambiguity. I hope that in your time here you have come across the name of John Henry Faulk. He was a great storyteller, a great entertainer. He was a man of virtue. Because of his celebrity status in the entertainment world of the fifties, he was forced into an ethical dilemma: Give the United States government the names of friends and colleagues who might have Communist leanings, and we will allow you to continue to make your livelihood telling stories and entertaining us. If you don't, you will be black-listed and will not work for a major network again. John Henry Faulk did not compromise principle and paid the price of an obstructed career and financial hardship. It was a decision he never regretted, even in his lowest moments.

Anita Hill faced an ethical dilemma. She knew that to testify against Clarence Thomas with the kind of anecdotes and evidence she possessed would mean subjecting herself to the most scurrilous and wicked humor of which petty minds are capable. Yet she testified. Some may view the results of her testimony as a loss. Clarence Thomas is on the Supreme Court. But she made the subject of sexual harassment infinitely more visible and has made it easier for women—and men—of lesser public stature to raise the issues of harassment in the workplace with much less fear of improper reprisals.

I do not know what the future holds for you. But I have every confidence in your abilities and in the preparation you are receiving here at this institution. Immediate success in your chosen field will not automatically bestow upon you the qualities of leadership. You must begin now—if you haven't already—to draw the parameters for the ethical content of your life.

Each of us faces ethical dilemmas in our everyday life, no matter how glamorous or how pedestrian that life might be. You may have read William Styron's book *Sophie's Choice* or seen that movie. Sophie was no Abraham, yet her fictional ethical dilemma was just as excruciating as Abraham's. Could you face the decision of which of your children to take with you into forced hard labor and which to send to a certain death?

As a student, what is your moral and ethical obligation if you see a classmate, even a friend, cheating on an exam or a research project? If you are a journalist, under what, if any, circumstances do you reveal the source of a story when you have promised to keep that identity secret? If you are an attorney, do you betray your profession's code of ethics and your client at the request of a prosecutor or judge seeking information that you might hold? If you are the owner of a small business that has environmental impacts beyond the borders of your property, do you locate in a low-income or minority area where opposition to such businesses has traditionally had little political sway?

As you exercise your leadership roles here on the university campus—as you graduate and move on to careers and aspire to assume leadership roles in your professions, your communities, and perhaps broader arenas—I suggest that it is important to understand that even your seemingly incidental ethical choices are setting the patterns for your life.

Benjamin Spock wrote a volume called *Decent and Indecent: Our Personal and Political Behavior*. His major conclusion? "I found that it is impossible to shuck one's character." It is impossible to shuck one's character. You are making the choices today that are shaping your lives. The pulls and tugs on you are intense. You are still caught between your parents' values and your desire to achieve independence from those values—whether your parents are the greatest or not!

You are caught between your individual values, beliefs, morals, ethics, and those that have been accepted by a majority of your peers. I do not intend this to insult your youth. To the contrary, I delight in youth and find daily challenges and inspiration in my students. Your ethical core with all of its concepts is not yet locked into place. You are still maturing and developing. You are still determining whether you will gravitate more toward the intellect or more toward the heart. Which will be your primary governor—head or heart?

It is critical for you as current and future leaders to develop that ethical core. I refer to Benjamin Spock again because of something he said which gives voice to an idea with which I agree. He said, "I have come to realize that the worst problems in America—illegal war, racial injustice, unnecessary poverty, for example—are caused not by lack of knowledge or means but by moral blindness or confusion. So I have come full circle, to a feeling that it is crucial, in all issues, to consider the moral dimension."

There are ethical dilemmas in leadership. You may be armed with all the facts and all of the latest management theories, but unless you consider the moral dimension, I contend that your decisions and your leadership will be hollow right down to the core.

And how do you consider the moral dimension? How do you prepare yourself—other than being more keenly aware that how you make your daily, personal decisions is shaping your framework for making more global decisions—how do you prepare yourself for leadership?

I have spoken more than once about what I call *conviction values*. By that, I mean that one should have some principles, ethics, or standards that are firmly fixed, unwavering and immutable; that there are some traits of character that are, or should be, nonnegotiable; that we should have a set of beliefs that is endemic to our concept of self.

Do not let me mislead you. I do *not* mean values that cause one to be rigid, inflexible, and unwilling to compromise when compromise is necessary. Nor are all conviction values necessarily good. If such values are antithetical to basic human rights and to maximizing hope, they should be rejected.

I offer to you the idea that our conviction values should foster a sense of community and be healing and civilizing. They are not fancy concepts. They are represented by such ordinary words as education, loyalty, honesty, kindness, justice, and responsibility.

I offer education as a conviction value because it should be both a value of the individual and of the whole society. As Texas has agonized for too many years now over the idea of equitably funding public education, it should have become clear to us that education is a value that helps both the student and the community.

But you are some of the best and the brightest. I think you have the capacity to develop your own list in a meaningful way. You have the freedom to choose the kind of future you want. You are denied the luxury of opting out. You can't. You are already involved with life.

One of my ethics students, Andrea Guerrero, wrote a paper in which she first presented a poem by Martin Carter, a Guyanese poet. That poem eloquently states my concluding words to you. The poem:

> You are involved
> This I have learnt
> Today a speck
> Tomorrow a hero
> Hero or monster
> You are consumed
> Like a jig
> Shakes the loom
> Like a web
> Is spun the pattern
> All are involved
> All are consumed.

Thank you for listening.

Famous Speeches

Of the many requests and questions we are asked in the Jordan Archives, the most numerous requests are for Jordan's two keynote addresses that were delivered at the Democratic National Party Conventions, as well as her Senate Judiciary Hearings Speech. The question we are most often asked is, why did Barbara Jordan retire from politics? Following are her most often requested speeches plus the statement she gave *Time* magazine when she decided not to seek another term in Congress.

What the people want is simple. They want an America as good as its promise.

Harvard University Commencement Address
JUNE 16, 1977

Democratic National Convention Address

One hundred and forty years ago, members of the Democratic Party met for the first time in convention to select their presidential candidate. Since that time, Democrats have continued to convene once every four years to draft a party platform and nominate a presidential candidate. Our meeting this week continues that tradition.

There is something different and special about this opening night. I am a keynote speaker. In the intervening years since 1832, it would have been most unusual for any national political party to have asked a Barbara Jordan to make a keynote address—most unusual.

The past notwithstanding, a Barbara Jordan is before you tonight. This is one additional bit of evidence that the American Dream need not forever be deferred.

Now that I have this distinction, what should I say? I could easily spend this time praising the accomplishments of this party and attacking the record of the Republicans. I do not choose to do that.

I could list the many problems which cause people to feel cynical, frustrated, and angry: problems which include the lack of integrity in government, the feeling that the individual no longer counts, the realities of material and spiritual poverty, the feeling that the grand American experiment is failing—or has failed. Having described these and other problems, I could sit down without offering any solutions. I do not choose to do that either.

The citizens of America expect more. They deserve and want more than a recital of problems. We are a people in a quandary about the present and in search of our future. We are a people in search of a national community. It is a search that is unending, for we are not only trying to solve the problems of the moment—inflation, unemployment—but on a larger scale, we are attempting to fulfill the promise of America. We are attempting to fulfill our national purpose, to create and sustain a society in which all of us are equal.

Throughout our history, when the people have looked for new ways to uphold the principles upon which this nation rests, they have turned to the political parties. Often they have turned to the Democratic Party.

What is it about the Democratic Party that has made it the instrument through which the people have acted to shape their future? The answer is our concept of governing, which is derived from our view of people. It is a concept rooted in a set of beliefs that are firmly etched in our national consciousness.

What are these beliefs?

First, we believe in equality for all and privileges for none. It is a belief that each American, regardless of background, has equal standing in the public forum. Because we believe in this idea, we are an inclusive rather than an exclusive party. I think it no accident that most of those emigrating to America during the nineteenth century identified with the Democratic Party. We are a heterogeneous party, made up of Americans with diverse backgrounds.

We believe that the people are the source of governmental power, that the authority of the people is to be extended rather than restricted. This can be accomplished only by providing each citizen with every opportunity to participate in the management of the government.

We believe that the government, which represents the authority of *all* the people—not just one interest group, but all the people—has an obligation to *actively* seek to remove those obstacles that block individual achievement: obstacles emanating from race, sex, and economic condition.

We are the party of innovation. We do not reject our traditions, but are willing to adapt to changing circumstances. We are willing to suffer the discomfort of change in order to achieve a better future. We have a positive vision of the future founded on our belief that the gap between the reality and the promise of America can be closed. This is the bedrock of our concept of governing—the reasons why Americans have turned to the Democratic Party. These are the foundations upon which a national community can be built.

Let all understand that these guiding principles cannot be discarded for short-term political gain, for they are indigenous to the American idea. They represent what this country is all about. They are not negotiable.

In other times, this exposition of our beliefs would have been sufficient reason for the majority to vote for the nominees of the Democratic Party. Such is not the case today. We have made mistakes. We admit them. In our haste to do all things for all people, we did not foresee the full consequences of our actions, and when the people raised their voices in protest, we did not listen. Our deafness was only a temporary condition and not an irreversible one.

Yet, even as I admit that we have made mistakes, I still believe that as the American people sit in judgment on each party, they will realize that ours were mistakes of the heart.

Now we must look to the future. Let us heed the voice of the people and recognize their common sense. If we do not, we not only blaspheme our political heritage, we also ignore the common ties that bind Americans. Many fear the future's uncertainty, are distrustful of their leaders, and believe that their voices are not heard. Many seek only to satisfy their private dreams. They ignore the common interest—the common good.

This is the great danger that America faces, that we will cease to be one nation and become instead a collection of interest groups, each seeking to fulfill private dreams, each seeking to satisfy private wants.

If this occurs, who then will speak for America? Who will speak for the common good? This is the question to be answered in 1976.

Are we to be one people bound together by a common spirit, sharing in a common endeavor, or will we become a divided nation: region versus region, city versus suburb, interest group against interest group and neighbor against neighbor?

For all of its uncertainty, we cannot flee from the future. We cannot become the new puritans and *reject* our society. We must address and master the future together. It can be done if we restore the belief that we share a common national endeavor, if we restore our sense of national community.

No executive order can require us to form this national community. No federal law can require us to uphold the common good. This we must do as individuals. It will thus be veto-proof.

As a first step, we must restore our belief in ourselves. We are a generous people. Let us be generous with each other and *take to heart* the words spoken by Thomas Jefferson:

> Let us restore to social intercourse that harmony and affection without which liberty and even life are but dreary things.

A nation is formed by the willingness of each of us to share in the responsibility for upholding the common good. A government is invigorated when each of us is willing to participate in the shaping of its future.

In this election year, when we must define the common good and begin again to shape our common future, let each person do his or her part. If one citizen is unwilling to participate, we all suffer, for the American idea, though shared by all, is realized in each one of us.

Those of us who are public servants must set the example. It is hypocritical for us to exhort the people to fulfill their duty to the republic if we are derelict in ours. More is required of us than slogans, handshakes, and press releases. We must hold ourselves strictly accountable.

If we promise, we must deliver. If we propose, we must produce. If we ask for sacrifice, we must be the first to give. If we make mistakes, we must be willing to admit them.

We must provide the people with a vision of the future that is attainable. We must strike a balance between the idea that the government can do everything and the belief that the government should do nothing.

Let there be no illusions about the difficulty of forming this national community. A spirit of harmony can only survive if each of us remembers, when bitterness and self-interest seem to prevail, that we share a common destiny.

I have confidence that we can form a national community. I have confidence that the Democratic Party *can* lead the way. We cannot improve on the system of government handed down to us by the founders of the republic, but we can find new ways to implement that system and to realize our destiny.

At the beginning of my remarks, I commented about the uniqueness of a Barbara Jordan speaking to you on this night. I shall conclude by quoting a Republican President and asking you to relate the words of Abraham Lincoln to the concept of a national community in which every last one of us participates:

> As I would not be a slave, so I would not be a master. This expresses my idea of democracy. Whatever differs from this, to the extent of the difference is no democracy.

Change: From What to What?

At this time, at this place, at this event sixteen years ago—I presented a keynote address. I thank you for the return engagement and with modesty would remind you that we *won* the presidency in November 1976. Why not 1992?

It is possible to win. It is possible, but you must believe that we can and will do it. I will talk with you for the next few minutes about some of the changes which are necessary for victory. I have titled my remarks "Change: From What to What?"

Change has become the watchword of this year's electioneering. Candidates contend with each other, arguing, debating—which of them is the authentic agent of change. Such jostling acquires substance when we comprehend the public mind.

There appears to be a general apprehension about the future which undermines our confidence in ourselves and each other. The American idea that tomorrow will be better than today has become destabilized by a stubborn, sluggish economy. Jobs lost have become permanent unemployment rather than cyclical unemployment. Public policy makers are held in low regard. Mistrust abounds. Given such an environment, is it not understandable that the prevailing issue of this political season is identifying the catalyst for change that is required? I see that catalyst as the Democratic Party and its nominee for President.

We are not strangers to change. We calmed the national unrest in the wake of the Watergate abuses and we, the Democratic Party, can seize this moment. We know what needs to be done and how to do it. We have been the instrument of change in policies which impact education, human rights, civil rights, economic and social opportunity, and the environment. These are policies firmly imbedded in the soul of our party. We will do nothing to erode our essence. However, some things need to change. The Democratic Party is alive and well. It will change in order to faithfully serve the present and the future, but it will not die.

Change: From What to What? We will change from a party with a reputation of tax and spend to one of investment and growth. A growth economy is a must. We can expand the economy and at the same time sustain and even improve our environment. When the economy is growing and we are treating our air, water, and soil kindly, *all* of us prosper. We all benefit from economic expansion. I certainly do not mean the thinly disguised racism and elitism of some kind of trickle-down economics. I mean an economy where a young Black woman or man from the Fifth Ward in Houston or south-central Los Angeles, or a young person in the *colonias* of the lower Rio Grande Valley, can attend public schools and learn the skills that will enable her or him to prosper. We must have an economy that does not force the migrant worker's child to miss school in order to earn less than the minimum wage just so the family can have one meal a day. That is the moral bankruptcy that trickle-down economics is all about. We can change the direction of America's economic engine and become proud and competitive again. The American Dream is not dead. True, it is gasping for breath, but it is not dead. However, there is no time to waste, because the American Dream is slipping away from too many. It is slipping away from too many Black and brown mothers and their children, from the homeless of every color and sex, from the immigrants living in communities without water and sewer systems. The American Dream is slipping away from the workers whose jobs are no longer there because we are better at building war equipment that sits in warehouses than we are at building decent housing, from the workers on indefinite layoffs while their chief executive officers are making bonuses that are more than the worker will take home in ten or twenty or thirty years.

We need to change the decaying inner cities into places where hope lives. We should answer Rodney King's haunting question "Can we all get along?" with a resounding "YES." We must profoundly change from the deleterious environment of the eighties, characterized by greed, selfishness, megamergers, and debt overhand, to one characterized by devotion to the public interest and tolerance. And yes, love.

We are one, we Americans, and we reject any intruder who seeks to divide us by race or class. We honor cultural identity. However, separatism is not allowed. Separatism is not the American way. And we should not permit ideas like political correctness to become some fad that could reverse our hard-won achievements in civil rights and human rights. Xenophobia has no place in the Democratic Party. We seek to unite people, not divide them, and we reject both white racism and Black racism. This party will not tolerate bigotry under any guise. America's strength is rooted in its diversity.

Our history bears witness to that statement. *E pluribus unum* was a good motto in the early days of our country and it is a good motto today. From the many, one. It still identifies us—because we are Americans.

We must frankly acknowledge our complicity in the creation of the unconscionable budget deficit and recognize that to seriously address it will put entitlements at risk. The idea of justice between generations mandates such acknowledgment and more. The baby boomers and their progeny have a right to a secure future. We must be willing to sacrifice for growth—provided there is equity in sacrifice. Equity means all will sacrifice—equally. That includes the retiree living on a fixed income, the day laborer, the corporate executive, the college professor, the member of Congress—all means all.

One overdue change already under way is the number of women challenging the councils of political power dominated by white-male policy makers. That horizon is limitless. What we see today is simply a dress rehearsal for the day and time we meet in convention to nominate . . . Madame President.

This country can ill afford to continue to function using less than half of its human resources, brain power, and kinetic energy. Our nineteenth-century visitor from France, de Tocqueville, observed in his work *Democracy in America*, "If I were asked to what singular substance do I mainly attribute the prosperity and growing strength of the American people, I should reply: to the superiority of their women." The twentieth century will not close without our presence being keenly felt.

We must leave this convention with a determination to convince the American people to trust us, the Democrats, to govern again. That is not an easy task, but it is a doable one.

Public apprehension and fears about the future have provided fertile ground for a chorus of cynics. Their refrain is that it makes no difference who is elected President. Advocates of that point of view perpetuate a fraud. It does make a difference who is President. A Democratic President would appoint a Supreme Court Justice who would protect liberty, not burden it. A Democratic President would promote those policies and programs which help us help ourselves, such as health care and job training.

Character has become an agenda item this political season. A well-reasoned examination of the question of character reveals more emotionalism than fact. James Madison warned us of the perils of acting out of passion rather than reason. When reason prevails, we prevail. As William Allen White, the late editor of the Emporia, Kansas, *Gazette*, said, "Reason never has failed man. Only fear and oppression have made the wrecks in the world." It is reason and not passion which should guide our decisions. The question persists: Who can best lead this country at this moment in our history?

I close by quoting from Franklin Roosevelt's first inaugural address to a people longing for change from the despair of the Great Depression. That was 1933. He said: "In every dark hour of our national life a leadership of frankness and vigor has met with that understanding and support of the people themselves which is essential to victory." Given the ingredients of today's national environment, maybe—just maybe—we Americans are poised for a second "rendezvous with destiny."

Testimony Before the House Judiciary Committee (Watergate)

Peter Rodino: I recognize the gentlelady from Texas, Ms. Jordan, for the purpose of general debate, not to exceed a period of fifteen minutes.

Ms. Jordan: Thank you, Mr. Chairman. Mr. Chairman, I join my colleague, Mr. Rangel, in thanking you for giving the junior members of this committee the glorious opportunity of sharing the pain of this inquiry. Mr. Chairman, you are a strong man and it has not been easy, but we have tried as best we can to give you as much assistance as possible.

Earlier today, we heard the beginning of the Preamble to the Constitution of the United States. "We, the people." It is a very eloquent beginning. But when that document was completed on the 17th of September in 1787, I was not included in that "We, the people." I felt somehow for many years that George Washington and Alexander Hamilton just left me out by mistake. But through the process of amendment, interpretation, and court decision, I have finally been included in "We, the people."

Today, I am an inquisitor. I believe hyperbole would not be fictional and would not overstate the solemnness that I feel right now. My faith in the Constitution is whole; it is complete; it is total. I am not going to sit here and be an idle spectator to the diminution, the subversion, the destruction of the Constitution.

"Who can so properly be the inquisitors for the nation as the representatives of the nation themselves?" (Hamilton, *Federalist Papers*, No. 65). The subject of its jurisdiction are those offenses which proceed from the misconduct of public men. That is what we are talking about. In other words, the jurisdiction comes from the abuse or violation of some public trust. It is wrong, I suggest; it is a misreading of the Constitution for any member here to assert that for a member to vote for an Article of Impeachment means that that member must be convinced that the President should be removed from office. The Constitution doesn't say that. The powers relating to impeachment are an essential check in the hands of this body, the legislature, against and upon the encroachment of the Executive. In establishing the division between the two branches of the legislature, the House and the Senate, assigning to the one the right to accuse and to the other the right to judge, the Framers of this Constitution were very astute. They did not make the accusers and the judges the same person.

We know the nature of impeachment. We have been talking about it awhile now. "It is chiefly designated for the President and his high ministers" to somehow be called into account. It is designed to "bridle" the Executive if he engages in excesses. "It is designed as a method of national inquest into the conduct of public men" (Hamilton, *Federalist Papers*, No. 65). The Framers confined in the Congress the power, if need be, to remove the President in order to strike a delicate balance between a President swollen with power and grown tyrannical, and preservation of the independence of the Executive. The nature of impeachment is a narrowly channeled exception to the separation of powers maxim; the Federal Convention of 1787 said that. It limited impeachment to high crimes and misdemeanors and discounted and opposed the term "maladministration." "It is to be used only for great misdemeanors," so it was said in the North Carolina Ratification Convention. And in the Virginia Ratification Convention: "We do not trust our liberty to a particular branch. We need one branch to check the others." The North Carolina Ratification Convention: "No one need be afraid that officers who commit oppression will pass with immunity."

"Prosecutions of impeachments will seldom fail to agitate the passions of the whole community," said Hamilton in the *Federalist Papers*, No. 65, "and to divide it into parties, more or less friendly or inimical to the accused." I do not mean political parties in that sense.

The drawing of political lines goes to the motivation behind impeachment, but impeachment must proceed within the confines of the constitutional term "high crimes and misdemeanors."

Of the impeachment process, it was Woodrow Wilson who said that "Nothing short of the grossest of offenses against the plain law of the land will suffice to give them speed and effectiveness. Indignation so great as to overgrow party interest may secure a conviction; nothing else can."

Common sense would be revolted if we engaged upon this process for petty reasons. Congress has a lot to do: appropriations, tax reform, health insurance, campaign finance reform, housing, environmental protection, energy sufficiency, mass transportation. Pettiness cannot be allowed to stand in the face of such overwhelming problems. So today we are not being petty. We are trying to be big because the task we have before us is a big one.

This morning in a discussion of the evidence, we were told that the evidence which purports to support the allegations of misuse of the CIA by the President is thin. We are told that that evidence is insufficient. What that recital of the evidence this morning did not include is what the President did know on June 23, 1972. The President did know that it was Republican money, that which was found in the possession of one of the burglars arrested on June 17.

What the President did know on the 23rd of June was the prior activities of E. Howard Hunt, which included his participation in the break-in of Daniel Ellsberg's psychiatrist, which included Howard Hunt's participation in the Dita Beard ITT affair, which included Howard Hunt's fabrication of cables designed to discredit the Kennedy Administration.

We were further cautioned today that perhaps these proceedings ought to be delayed because certainly there would be new evidence forthcoming from the President of the United States. There has not even been an obfuscated indication that this committee would receive any additional materials from the President. The committee subpoena is outstanding and if the President wants to supply that material, the committee sits here.

The fact is that on yesterday, the American people waited with great anxiety for eight hours, not knowing whether their President would obey an order of the Supreme Court of the United States.

At this point, I would like to juxtapose a few of the impeachment criteria with some of the President's actions.

[On] impeachment criteria, James Madison, from the Virginia Ratification Convention: "If the President be connected in any suspicious manner with any person and there be grounds to believe that he will shelter him, he may be impeached."

We have heard time and time again that the evidence reflects payment to the defendants of money. The President had knowledge that these funds were being paid and these were funds collected for the 1972 presidential campaign.

We know that the President met with Mr. Henry Petersen twenty-seven times to discuss matters related to Watergate and immediately thereafter met with the very persons who were implicated in the information Mr. Petersen was receiving and transmitting to the President. The words are "If the President be connected in any suspicious manner with any person and there be grounds to believe that he will shelter that person, he may be impeached."

Justice Story: "Impeachment is intended for occasional and extraordinary cases where a superior power acting for the whole people is put into operation to protect their rights and rescue their liberties from violation."

We know about the Huston Plan. We know about the break-in of the psychiatrist's office. We know that there was absolute, complete direction in August 1971 when the President instructed Ehrlichman to "do whatever is necessary." This instruction led to a surreptitious entry into Dr. Fielding's office.

"Protect their rights." "Rescue their liberties from violation."

The South Carolina Ratification Convention impeachment criteria: Those are impeachable "who behave amiss or betray their public trust."

Beginning shortly after the Watergate break-in and continuing to the present time, the President has engaged in a series of public statements and actions designed to thwart the lawful investigation by government prosecutors. Moreover, the President has made public announcements and assertions bearing on the Watergate case which the evidence will show he knew to be false.

These assertions, false assertions, impeachable, those who misbehave. Those who "behave amiss or betray their public trust."

James Madison, again, at the Constitutional Convention: "A President is impeachable if he attempts to subvert the Constitution."

The Constitution charges the President with the task of taking care that the laws be faithfully executed, and yet he disregarded the secrecy of grand jury proceedings, concealed surreptitious entry, attempted to compromise a federal judge while publicly displaying his cooperation with the processes of criminal justice.

"A President is impeachable if he attempts to subvert the Constitution."

If the impeachment provision in the Constitution of the United States will not reach the offenses charged here, then perhaps the eighteenth-century Constitution should be abandoned to a twentieth-century paper shredder. Has the President committed offenses and planned and directed and acquiesced in a course of conduct which the Constitution will not tolerate? That is the question. We know that. We know the question. We should now forthwith proceed to answer the question. It is reason, not passion, which must guide our deliberations, guide our debate, and guide our decision.

I yield back the balance of my time, Mr. Chairman.

Statement Given to *Time* Magazine on Retirement from Congress

On December 10, 1971, I first announced my candidacy for election to the United States House of Representatives. On December 10, 1977, I announced that I would not seek a fourth term in the House. During the five years I have served in the Congress, my time has seemingly been exclusively devoted to representing the people of the Eighteenth Congressional District of Texas, people who, heretofore, I hoped would see fit to return me to office. The demands on the time of a member of Congress, at least this member, permit precious little time for personal refreshment and reflection. Those demands and that piece of time will conclude when my current term expires in January 1979. My decision not to seek reelection was not made hastily nor will I decide hastily about the course (or courses) I shall pursue in 1979. My decision was based solely on what became the conviction that I wanted to do something different.

I will leave the Congress with no regrets for having served there and with a profound and lasting respect for the institution. Congress was not, I believe, intended to be a haven for life. The founders did not contemplate longevity of service as the benchmark of congressional accomplishment. Quite the contrary. James Madison believed the limitation of the term of appointment was necessary for protection of the common good. In the *Federalist Papers* No. 57, he wrote:

> The aim of every political constitution is, or ought to be, first to obtain for rulers men who possess most wisdom to discern, and most virtue to pursue,

109

the common good of society, and in the next place, to take the most effectual precautions for keeping them virtuous whilst they continue to hold their public trust. The elective mode of obtaining rulers is the characteristic policy of republican government. The means relied on in this form of government for preventing their degeneracy are numerous and various. The most effectual one is such a limitation on the term of appointments as will maintain a proper responsibility to the people.

By endorsing those thoughts of Madison, I do not suggest a mandatory limitation of the term of office. I only suggest that there should be nothing unusual or baffling about voluntarily limiting the terms of appointment.

It would appear that there is widespread belief that Congress is lumbersome. It is. Over 200 million people have said to 535 people, "Go to Washington and make my life better. Specifically, I want you to establish justice, ensure domestic tranquility, provide for the defense of the nation, promote the general welfare, and secure liberty." That is a big order. In trying to fill it, Congress is sometimes clumsy and inarticulate. Even so, the republic has survived remarkably well.

The basic charge to the member of Congress has not changed since the founding of the republic: to represent. The nature of the job has changed. As the country has moved from the simple to the complex, so have the issues with which the Congress must deal. Events have forced the country's attention to move from the danger of entangling alliances (George Washington's admonishment) to the United Nations and NATO, from the naiveté of isolation to leadership of the free world, from an individually centered market economy to corporations to conglomerates, from rugged individualism to the necessity for interdependence. "Street talk" now includes neutron bombs and cybernetics. The budget of the First Congress for the biennium 1789–1791 was $4,000,269. Receipts were $4,419,000. The budget for fiscal year 1978 is $458.3 billion. Projected receipts are $397 billion with the resulting deficit of $61.3 billion. Extraordinary flexibility and a capacity to learn and to listen are qualities which outstanding members have in common. A responsible member must deal with a complicated set of facts knowledgeably and expeditiously.

Given the complexity and diversity of the issues, one might conclude that longevity in office would enhance the knowledge and professionalism of the officeholder. I do not agree. The issues with which the member deals are so numerous and broad in scope that time available for study and the development of expertise are insufficient. Thus there is a heavy reliance on professional staff and the member is reduced to being a communication conduit for his or her constituents.

With the exceptions of ethnicity and sex, the members of Congress are reflective of the people of America. However, it seems that the public is of the persuasion that members of Congress qualify for office because of a special admissions program for the morally disadvantaged. In fact, the qualifications for office have not changed since the beginning. The Constitution specifies only age, citizenship, and residency requirements and speaks to the subject of conduct in office in only one sentence: "Each House may determine the rules of proceedings, punish its Members for disorderly behavior and, with the concurrence of two-thirds, expel a Member." My experience causes me to believe that members are frequently and undeservedly maligned. It is my belief that members of Congress are more mindful of being surrogates of the people than is commonly believed.

Whether or not public office is a high calling is dependent only, I believe, on the integrity of the officeholder, not on opinion polls. Good government requires good people—people who are mindful of America's heritage and what this country is about.

1977. Photo by Kit Brooking. Reprinted by permission of Texas Southern University Archives.